In the Act: Essays on the Poetry of Hayden Carruth

Edited by David Weiss

A Twentieth-Anniversary Special Edition
of Seneca Review

Hobart and William Smith Colleges Press, Geneva, New York, 1990

SENECA REVIEW VOL. XX, No. 1

Twentieth Anniversary Special Edition

EDITOR
Deborah Tall

GUEST EDITOR FOR THIS ISSUE
David Weiss

FOUNDING EDITORS
James Crenner
Ira Sadoff

CONTRIBUTING EDITORS
Donald Hall
Barbara Harlow
David Weiss

ASSISTANT EDITOR
Jennifer Corse

MANAGING EDITOR
Tamar March

CIRCULATION MANAGER
Sharon Elder

COVER DESIGN
Gwen Butler
Photograph by Juliana Thaens

Hayden Carruth's sonnets are reprinted here by permission of The Press of Appletree Alley.

Seneca Review is published semi-annually by Hobart and William Smith Colleges, Geneva, NY 14456. Subscriptions are $8 per year, $15 for 2 years. Single copies of current or available back issues are $5 each.

Unsolicited manuscripts of poetry and criticism of contemporary poetry are read annually between September 1st and May 1st. Manuscripts sent at other times will be returned unread. No manuscripts can be returned unless accompanied by a stamped, self-addressed envelope.

Poems published in *Seneca Review* are indexed in *Index of American Periodical Verse, Annual Index to Poetry in Periodicals,* and *American Humanities Index.*

Full Index to back issues available on request.

Library of Congress National Series Data Program ISSN 0037-2145.

Twentieth anniversary special edition, ISBN 0-934888-14-0.

Copyright © 1990 by Hobart and William Smith Colleges.

Printed by IPS MacDonald, Rochester, NY.

CONTENTS

Introduction 5
Hayden Carruth
   Sonnets 7
Philip Booth
   A Few Riffs for Hayden, Sitting in With His Horn 14
Wendell Berry
   A Poem of Difficult Hope 16
Geof Hewitt
   New Wind for Old Farts: An Essay on Suffering Fools 22
W. S. Di Piero
   On Hayden Carruth 26
David Rivard
   A Meaning of Hayden Carruth 30
Maxine Kumin
   On "North Winter" 47
David Weiss
   Taking Sides 50
Anthony Robbins
   Hyperborean Necessities: On From Snow and Rock,
     From Chaos: Poems 1965–1972 60
Stephen Kuusisto
   Elegiac Locales: The Anarchy of Hayden Carruth 75
Sam Hamill
   Listening In 83
William Matthews
   The Poetry Blues 92
Geoffrey Gardner
   Homage to the One-Man Band with Incredible Ears 97
Carolyn Kizer
   Others Call it God 106
David Budbill
   When You Use Your Head, Your Ears Fall Off:
     My Twenty Years of Listening to Music with the
     Supernumerary Cockroach 113
David Weiss
   An Interview with Hayden Carruth 128

INTRODUCTION

At the inception of this project, I asked Hayden Carruth about some lines of a poem from his most recent collection:

> ... I had once written
> Poems to be read many times, but what was the use of that? Now
> I write poems to be read once and forgotten,
> Or not to be read at all.

They had unsettled me and seemed out of keeping with his own attitudes. *Yes, I believed that and still do,* he replied. *There is no real audience now beyond the university. I write now for two or three friends who may admire my poems but who will not fundamentally be affected by them. This is very painful to me. I have never believed in poetry for poetry's sake. But now I think of my poems as flowers, born in a day, gone in a day.* This is a paraphrase of what he said. The tape recorder went haywire that day, but his bitterness was clear.

I argued with Hayden, although not about the state of our culture, hardly arguable. I said that his poems have been important to me; at a certain troubled moment in my life, they made it possible to keep writing. His career said to me that one's identity as a poet is not synonymous with homogeneity of style. His poems gave proof that idiosyncracy, the overt expression of ideas, intentional awkwardness, heterogeneousness of tone and diction within a single poem, complexity of rhythm and syntax, could all be managed with directness and strength of feeling. His work made clear that the wholeness and beauty of a poem may, even must, reside in a surprising harmony. I didn't say all this, of course, only that his poems had made a difference to me beyond any simple admiration. He nodded in grum acknowledgement.

The essays gathered here may be more persuasive than my remonstrations. They express a debt—a freedom, really—that many owe to the poems and prose and to Carruth himself. What's striking is how many of the essays, particularly among those by younger poets (Gardner, Di Piero, Robbins, Rivard, Hamill, Kuusisto and myself), testify to his influence, a broad and protective and countenancing one. No poet is less imitable than Hayden Carruth.

Yet his work evinces and points to a subjectivity greater than mere egotism, to a speaking self that's truer the more inclusive it gets, and to a broader and riskier range of poetic resources than most of his contemporaries, poets born in the 1920's. Spontaneous similarities among many of these essays bespeak the ways Carruth has been important to other poets. Certain notions recur, and particular poems, like touchstones, are quoted with frequency, yet in each instance viewed from a different angle of concern. There are, in addition, reminiscences by Geof Hewitt and David Budbill, Vermont neighbors of Carruth, a poem for him by Philip Booth, and pieces by his compeers, Wendell Berry, Maxine Kumin, William Matthews, and Carolyn Kizer. You will find at the head of this volume thirteen new sonnets by Carruth reprinted from a limited edition by The Press of Appletree Alley and, at the back, an interview which did stick to the tape.

—David Weiss

Hayden Carruth

from *Sonnets*

1

In the mind of the kiss occurs a thought so rich
that it exonerates the astonished philosophers.
Ah well, we say, something beyond converse
of systems is working after all, in which
nothing is absolute, never that, but pitch
by tone by timbre (or every his by hers)
includes all musics, all visions, and so refers
both ways deep and deep to the farthest niche
of being. The kiss is one and is egoless,
free and undetermined; the two exist
in its intelligence, original and new,
knowing more than they know in their access
of single subjectivity. Van Gogh once kissed
a cypress tree, and I have once kissed you.

5

From our very high window at the Sheraton
in Montreal, amazed I stood a long time
gazing at Cosmopolis outward and down
in all its million glitterings, I who am
a countryman temerarious and lost
like our planet in the great galaxy,
one spark, one speck, one instant, yet the most
part of my thought was not displeasing to me,
but rather an excitement, a dare that could
still raise my pulse-rate after these sixty years
to exult in humanity so variable and odd
and burgeoning, so that bewildered tears
stood briefly in my eyes when we went to bed.
For hours we made love and the night sped.

11

Was Yahweh chosen by the chosen people?
I think so. Was their Covenant with themselves?
Of course. Did, as an animal kind evolves,
the god-idea begin with some apish couple
not risen yet to intellectual scruple
fucking in dark depression? How the wolves
howled in the night! How the flimsy valves
of the lovers' hearts gave way!
                            I'm an old cripple
dragging my mind like a clubfoot, but nothing comes
from nothing. Dearest, search as I will, age-proven,
back, back in imagination, still some given
is there, some glory in pandemonium's
gloom. Is it thus the great mind-light derives?
Cindy, in that god-glimmer we live our lives.

16

If I die today, which statistically speaking
is of greater likelihood than this man-child's
mind can readily grasp, please cart the leaking
bag of bones to the incineratorium that yields
a handful of dust, which scatter in the woods.
Not much humus will accrue, but at least a little.
No ceremonials. None. No specious interludes
in the public or private drinking. Pour a bottle
of brook-water for form's sake if some criticaster
demands libation. For monument, quite enough
to mount a stuffed crow on a rock, his posture
to indicate either alighting or taking off.
Then, Cindy, I don't know what you'll do.
I can't imagine. My heart goes out to you.

17

Avaunt, ye epigonoi! Avast, ye cruds and florians!
The School of Cannibalism is hereupon forfent!
What's left of me is Cindy's—and the historians'.
Please, please desist. If you've one unspent
nicklesworth of courtesy (though I recognize
the archaism of the concept), just go away.
The bad Herr Doktor has looked into my eyes
and pronounced his pronouncement. Do not say
your echolalia can give an old man wings.
Some maybe, but not this one. Your solemn faces,
burbling like goldfish at the surface of things,
groping for crumbs, are what disgraces
poetry. Cindy and I have gone to bed,
where I intend to remain until I'm dead!

22

Cindy, I've used my writing all my life
as the one inoffensive yet functional way
to escape what we agree no longer to try
describing, the System, and it's not enough;
my poems too are incorporated, taken off
to system-land, and everything they say
is co-opted. I hate to admit that that French boy,
Rimbaud, was right, but he was. And so I scoff,
mostly at myself, because weeping gets nowhere,
like writing, and there's not much else to do,
and anyway I'm too old. Let's let these few
poems left in me, long or short, "out there"
or "confessional," be just for us—not much
like writing, no, but more like a glance or a touch.

29

I want to do a complaint now. Which is to say
simply that a hypertrophied prostate,
whatever women and other such novices may
choose to believe, is quite precisely not
my idea of a *baba au rhum* at the Chez
Paul or a Sunday outing with the laureate
or a grandiluminarious sunset display
over the park, etc. Also it is somewhat
not like strawberry shortcake.
                                 On the contrary
it is that insidious, invidious last drip
which always waits, the inner adversary,
till I'm upzipped, helpless, and heading out, to slip
down my thigh like a seed of dying ice,
leaving a streak on my pants, which is not nice.

30

Today's word: autoclasticism. First my heart,
and now this high maddening screech in my ear,
relentless, originating somewhere
inside, I don't know where, except it's not
—not, I repeat—in that unapparent part
they taught me to call imagination. Stare
as I will, the mirror shows nothing but fear,
practiced anxiety. So life is short
and ripeness is all. I'm willing to conceive
that the value generated by this ill-endured
confrontation with the disintegrating Absurd
is what it means to be human and alive.
But still if it's all the same I think I'd rather
not come apart just when I've come together.

37

At first when hearing began to fail I thought
the world more frightening. I couldn't tell
from what direction noises came, yet that
is just what distinguishes them: churchbell
from struck crystal, bird from beast, thunder
from furnace, ambulance from vacuum cleaner,
and so forth. Clarity was gone. No wonder
I felt my life becoming, like my verses, meaner.
But is perception so important after all?
This morning I heard the wild geese in the sky.
I stepped out to find them. They were the shrill
kids on a playground several blocks away.
Tomorrow I'll *think* that I am hearing geese.
For a little while the world will be at peace.

39

Poor little book. *The Sleeping Beauty* died.
I mind one fall up on the mountainside
I found a cow, strayed – or perhaps denied,
I thought – a Guernsey with a scurfy hide
and bleeding feet, sharp-boned, rheumy-eyed,
who stood as if she half thought to confide
in men when I came near, although her pride
held her to herself. What would you do? I tried
to lead her home, and for a halter tied
my jacket-arms around her, but she shied
and would not. Next day was bright and wide
with new snow, but I found no trace of her
until, in June, white bones and scattered fur –
lost but for me, who would have been her guide.

46

To rebel. So I have saved my life, not once
but over and over these sixty years, and I'm
grateful to myself, of course. Epidemic time,
the bomb, gives any health a special importance.
Yet can it mean survival? This puppet dance
of outraged dignity, so theatrical, this mime
of Being, how futile! It asks more than rhyme,
not a changed self only, but changed existence,
and there is none. I don't know why rebellion
doesn't suffice. Maybe after all some given
in humanness, the "natural" dream of heaven,
drives us to hope, the one chance in a million.
But I give up. Comrades, you can have my books.
No longer will I throw poems at the fat archdukes.

51

You in a tallness slenderly, as a lone
white birch I knew once swaying in a small
wind, walk
        away from our bed to the window,
and in the light from the old streetlamp I am shown
the glisten of the line of the curve of the fall
from shoulder to flank, breast to knee,
                            in shadow
the gleam of the inner edges of your long legs
so that a wilderness in me, rising, begs
silently,
        and you turn, a calculus of bright
changing, glyphs in the dimness, and you walk
silently back, delicately, as the egrets stalk.
Truly, all things most good happen at night.
We know. Later with our last energy we talk
and fall asleep,
        embers of abeyant light.

55

If you see a child that shivers when it hears
a diminished fifth, nurture and protect him,
for he only in the schoolyard's fierce abstraction
will know the cry of the lynx, the cry of the hare,
and that of the old man and the young woman.
Shivering is his genius. If he have speech,
he will utter it greatly. If not, he will search
in other ways beyond the ordinarily human,
the hating and angered. He will hear the light,
he will sing the light and the darkness, or will sound
the ideas of them in the concrete nothingness
of tones vibrating in the air that sight
cannot conceive, yet they touch each one of us.
He will hear love where we would behold a wound.

Philip Booth

A Few Riffs for Hayden, Sitting in With His Horn

Been readin your book, thinkin
*T'aint what you say, it's
the way that you say it.* Been readin
your book, hearin your say.

Heard Oliver write that when I was young.
Never got over the way his horn sang.

I been seekin and failin all these last years.
I been seekin and failin all these last years.
Failin to give up, to give up old fears.
Seekin to wake up with true words to say,
wakin all night and sleepin all day.

Been readin your book, thinkin
it's good. Every note yours.
Been hearin you jam. Not
just good, plain better than.

T'aint just what you say, it's
the how that you say it:
the slow and the lonely, the hot
and the glad. Hayd, lemme tell you,
you got it bad. You hit right notes
and still make 'em want,
when you hit a wrong note
you let it go sad.

Though a while back I had it made.
Though I'd made it quite a while back.
Know now I never. Not even ever.
Only now startin, over and over.

You're in B flat in a world off key,
playin your sound, you say what you hear,
the cool and the hot notes, the slurred
and the held, the music
of being: old blues getting old.
With all of the All-Stars,
you're *Downbeat*'s main man.

After you've gone
you'll still be around.

Wendell Berry

A Poem of Difficult Hope

A poem by Hayden Carruth that I have returned to many times is the one entitled "On Being Asked to Write a Poem Against the War in Vietnam." The poem, in the guise of a refusal, responds directly to the invitation:

> Well I have and in fact
> more than one and I'll
> tell you this too
>
> I wrote one against
> Algeria that nightmare
> and another against
>
> Korea and another
> against the one
> I was in
>
> and I don't remember
> how many against
> the three
>
> when I was a boy
> Abyssinia Spain and
> Harlan County
>
> and not one
> breath was restored
> to one
>
> shattered throat
> mans womans or childs
> not one not

one
but death went on and on
never looking aside

except now and then like a child
with a furtive half-smile
to make sure I was noticing.

This poem obviously does not need explaining, and yet it presents a problem, first of understanding and then of criticism, that is unusual and difficult. I read the poem a good many times, I confess, before I was able to say why it interested me – before, that is, I was able to acknowledge the extent to which I am involved in and with its problem. The problem that the poet appears to be replying to is this: Why do something that you suspect, with reason, will do no good? And the poem appears to give, or to be, a negative reply: There is no use in doing it.

But after this refusal is given, the completed poem begins to imply its other, more important and more formidable question: What is the use of *saying* "There is no use"? The use, I think, depends on to whom and on how this denial is given.

In the first place, the distinguishing characteristic of absolute despair is silence. There is a world of difference between the person who, believing that there is no use, says so to himself or to no one, and the person who says it aloud to someone else. A person who marks his trail into despair remembers hope – and thus has hope, even if only a little. But if he speaks of despair, he must know it, and must speak as one who knows it. Speech about despair raises, the same as speech about anything else, the question of authenticity or honesty: How do we know he knows what he is talking about? And so we must, after all, examine the language and the making of this very plain and clear poem.

The thing we notice immediately is that the poem comes to us in the sound of a voice speaking. And here it is necessary to insist upon a distinction between verse written in "spoken" (as opposed to "literary") English, which may or may not have the qualities that lift verse into poetry, and verse that has the sound of a voice speaking, which does not necessarily have to be written in "spoken" English. The sound of a voice speaking, I think, often does have the power of lifting verse into poetry, for it is the quality that authenticates feeling. Hayden Carruth is a master in poetry of the speaking voice, whether the voice is his own or someone else's. This is not a matter of effects contrived out of diction and phraseology; I don't think it can be done that way. It is the result of technical skill so perfect and assured that it does not pause to admire itself, and therefore calls little attention to itself. The poem at hand is technically masterful, and its mastery, like that of a good cup or spoon, is unobtrusive; if not consciously looked for, it is not seen. But if we are looking, we see that the voice immediately characterizes the speaker. This voice is colloquial and cranky, absolutely direct, informed by feeling that has a history, and it has the courage to begin at full force. We know all this by the end of the first line, which gives us nothing but the quality of the voice: "Well I have and in fact ..." It is a line superbly cocked toward the declaration it leads into.

And this declaration is a single sentence, unpunctuated except for the period at the end. The absence of punctuation tends to collapse the several grammatical units into a single thrust of syntax through the divisions of lines and stanzas. We have only to look at Hayden Carruth's prose to suspect how much his poetic mastery is a mastery of syntax. Here is one of his prose sentences: "Verlaine, who in his life must be accounted among the most miserable of men, nevertheless had a steady, forthright mind." This is an unpretentious, useful sentence; it is also a masterful one, though, again, it has the modesty of authentic mastery. Only when we consciously examine it do we comment to ourselves on its balance, elegance, and discriminate exactitude. But when we say the sentence aloud or write it down, we *feel* all this immediately, and more besides. We feel also its wholeness as sense and as rhythmic pattern, and we feel the propriety of its length. The sentence's power is in its wholeness, its coherence, and it is a felt and a hearable wholeness. The sentence is sensible in both senses, as a sentence should be.

In this poem, Mr. Carruth has imposed upon the long breath of his powerful syntax the measures of lines and sentences, forcing it toward the heightened tension and the exacting stresses and halts of music. Thus we get the great beauty and pathos of the cadence "not one not // one," which written or spoken as prose is flat and uninteresting. The poem gets its power, coherence and momentum, from syntax, and it gets its precise emotional articulateness from the rhythmic divisions of line and stanza. This balance of power and exactitude authenticates the voice, which authenticates the statement. We feel that the poet knows what he is talking about because he is taking such palpable care to tell us exactly. The technical skill of this poem is the signature of the poet's concern to say what he has to say and to have it understood.

But we are now brought back more forcibly than ever to the odd and difficult question we started with: What is the use of saying "There is no use"? Obviously, the poet has not fallen into the silence of perfect despair, for he is speaking; and he is not talking only to himself, for he has published his poem. A use is thus clearly implied, but what is it? We can amplify the question a little to make it more precise, but in doing so we increase its apparent oddity: Why has this poet expended so much skill and care to tell us there is no use in doing what he has already done a number of times and is now, in fact, doing again? Is this a trick? One is tempted to ask, for it is impossible not to see that the poet, in the act of refusing to write a poem against the war, has written one.

It is, to say the least, an unusually complex protest poem. It is a poem that complicates our understanding of what political protest is and means. We fret and ponder over it so because in its astonishing simplicity it has placed us directly in the presence both of one of the bewilderments of our history and of one of the mysteries of our nature.

We are living in the most destructive and, hence, the most stupid period of the history of our species. The list of its undeniable abominations is long and hardly bearable. And these abominations are *not* balanced or compensated or atoned for by the list—endlessly reiterated—of our scientific achievements. Some people are moved, now and again, to protest one abomination or another. Others, and Hayden Carruth is one, protest the whole list and its causes. Much protest is naive; it expects quick, visible improvement, and despairs and gives up when such improvement does not come. Protesters who hold out longer are perhaps able to do so because they have understood that success is not the proper goal. If protest depended on success, then there would be little protest of any durability or significance. History simply affords too little evidence that anyone's individual protest is of any use. Protest that endures, I think, is moved by a hope far more modest than that of public success: namely, the hope of preserving qualities in one's own heart and spirit that would be destroyed by acquiescence.

A protest poem, then, had better confront not only the impossibility of restoring what has already been destroyed, but the likelihood that it will be unable to prevent further destruction. This, I take it, is simply one of the practicalities of political dissent and protest. And Mr. Carruth's poem takes up this practicality and makes music of it. He makes a protest poem that understands carefully the enforced, the inescapable, modesty of protest poems. And so his poem becomes necessarily more than a protest poem; it is also a lamentation for the dead who could not be saved, and for the poet who could not save them.

But something more is involved that is even harder to talk about because it is only slightly understandable, and that is the part that suffering plays in the economy of the spirit. It seems plain that the voice of our despair defines our hope exactly; it seems, indeed, that we cannot know of hope without knowing of despair, just as we know joy precisely to the extent that we know sorrow. Our culture contains much evidence of this, but one states it outright with some fear of giving justification to those dogmatic and violent people who undertake to do good by causing suffering. Is it necessary, as some appear to have supposed, to *cultivate* despair and sorrow in order to know hope and joy? No, for there will always be enough despair and sorrow. And what might have been the spiritual economy of Eden, when there was no knowledge of despair and sorrow? We don't need to worry about that.

What we do need to worry about is the possibility that we will be reduced, in the face of the enormities of our time, to silence or to mere protest. Mr. Carruth's protest poem is a poem against reduction. On its face, it protests — yet again — the reduction of the world, but its source is a profound instinct of resistance against the reduction of the poet and the man who is the poet. By its wonderfully sufficient artistry, the poem preserves the poet's wholeness of heart in the face of his despair. And it shows us how to do so as well. That we would help if we could means that we will help when we can.

Geof Hewitt

New Wind for Old Farts: An Essay on Suffering Fools

On the refrigerator door in the tiny kitchen of his year-round cottage in Johnson, Vermont, Hayden had taped a notice printed in his own hand, "NEW WIND FOR OLD FARTS: Because of the weight of paperwork that must be attended, the Old Fart will no longer accept phone calls or personal visits between 8 P.M. and 6 P.M. THIS MEANS YOU!" or something like that. It was 1976 and I was visiting at noon, catching Hayden still in his morning slippers and robe. It never occurred to me that the little notice might have been scribbled and taped to the wall only after my car was sighted on the pull-off between the dirt road and his cottage.

I was writing a book on self-employment and interviewed Hayden about his work as a writer. He patiently described the difference between the work he lives for and the work he takes for income. At the end of the interview, he pointed to a tumbling stack of letters, manuscripts and books from friends and admirers: "And that," he said, "represents the writing I do for neither of the two reasons we've discussed."

Hayden is a member of the old school, a gentleman in the sense that my father was a gentleman. A letter received, even an unsolicited letter, implies a commitment. I sometimes wonder what poems don't exist because Hayden takes this commitment so seriously. Then I stop to realize how many people have been touched by his sense of responsibility. I believe he has never falsely praised a fellow-writer, but if my review of his response to the manuscripts I mailed to him in the 1970's is any indication, he has always been gracious and honest simultaneously. His critiques sometimes suggested alternate phrasings, and always challenged assertions and implications that were not true in fact.

I have been the frequent recipient of Hayden's kindnesses and I continue to wonder how many other people share his generosity. Ten years ago I was young enough to believe that surely none but my own manuscripts were so happily received. How many other Vermont back-to-the-landers did Hayden nurture, how many people did he help butcher pigs and advise on garden matters and come help stack the wood and drive (because he had a truck) half a state's distance to pick up old windows someone offered for free? From coincidence I happen to know that Hayden has given his time to corresponding with at least one inmate on death row. I say "from coincidence" because this is not the sort of information he volunteers.

Hayden is a wonderful source of wisdom and a marvelous fountain of unlikely information and occasional misinformation, which, I believe, he sprinkles as a form of mischief that protects him from being labeled the complete sage. He once told me that a hen's comb turns snow white at the moment the egg passes through her cervix (or whatever it is called in hens), so I targeted my most docile Rhode Island Red, Mandy, for study and after learning her morning habits, appeared one Tuesday just as she was about to lay her egg and insinuated my hand between her raised rear and the little nest where, five or six days a week, she laid her morning egg. Dear Mandy looked me straight in the eye and never stopped heaving. I stared at her comb and when a steamy orb filled my hand and during all moments before and after that occurrence, Mandy's comb stayed red.

Without Hayden's assertion I'd never have learned that Mandy would lay right into my hand: long after I lost interest in the comb issue, I habituated the henhouse at 10 a.m. Tuesdays through Sundays in the hope that she would hop to the nest. I caught at least a dozen fresh eggs thanks to Hayden's bold claim which he continues to defend on the basis of personal experience.

What throws me off is that Hayden denies any ability at dissimulation. Early in our friendship, I pulled off the road into his little parking space when I saw him changing a tire. As he let the car off the jack onto the new tire, I made a subtle, persistent hissing sound. He cursed and, scowling, tried to reverse the direction of his jack, then laughed as I revealed the true source of the hiss. In conversations thereafter, he referred to that moment. "That's a brand of humor that would never occur to me. I'm too linear."

So three weeks later I'm standing in the henhouse with my hand under Mandy's ass.

Is it that he has suffered fools too long, or too long been asked his response to the same, tiring questions that he occasionally borders on the outrageous during question and answer sessions? After a reading at one university, he met with a large group of students, answering a variety of questions that might themselves be found outrageous in view that most answers lie in his poems.

What do you think of metaphorical images? "I don't like them. The idea that they are inherently poetic just because they spring from the imagination is extremely damaging. I agree with William Carlos Williams that objects in this world have their own identity. The human imagination can distort that by trying to bend them into metaphorical equivalences, but only at the risk of terrible effrontery. Yet how many people in this room write about the real objects in this world? How many of you have ever tried to write a poem about, say, a styrofoam cup?"

Do you have any specific advice for student writers? "There are simply too many poems about grandmothers right now. The topic is dead."

How about mothers? "Equally bad. And I will not read a poem that starts with the first person pronoun followed by a monosyllabic verb in the present tense. The present tense is all used up. When practically every student poem for the past thirty years has been in the present tense, you can see why I say that the present tense has had it. Further, there should be two tenses in every poem, I tell my students, and no personal pronouns are permissible until the second half of the poem. I wrote a book thirty years ago that has *no* personal pronouns and no one noticed but me. If you look back at the poetry of the eighteenth century you'll see few pronouns except objective pronouns like 'who' and 'what.' The nice thing about Latin is that the writer can get by without pronouns. A new kind of poetry for the twenty-first century will have to be developed or poetry may well die.

"A poet has to be perceptive with the ears. The idiom of a community changes with the community, and the poet has the challenge of hearing and recreating that idiom, using context and the poem's rhythms and relying on the reader's intelligence to capture what's happening. There is no way to write "well, all right" as we actually hear it every day in common speech – that slurred emphasis. Yet if we use it correctly in a poem, readers will know how to pronounce it.

"Incidentally, by far the best place to hear language is the emergency room of a hospital on a Saturday night – everyone is talking their head off."

I guess I like a reliable source of wisdom, natural speculation and occasionally outrageous assertion. I admire someone whose political beliefs are embodied in generosity and decency. It's marvelous that some poems occasion this public, personal and political activity, it's fortunate that a conscience and some mischief inform the same personality and it is unusual that someone who is a truly literate person can quietly accept both accolades and fawning requests, can meet with students to acknowledge discouragement and offer encouragement, can put a sign on the refrigerator door that no one is going to believe pertains to themselves.

W. S. Di Piero

On Hayden Carruth

I want to describe what Hayden Carruth has had to say about personality and poetry, and along the way say something about how his views helped to change my own thinking on the subject. He seems to have worked out his position—all his career he has taken care to articulate his position on important matters, not as polemical reflex but as provisional understanding kneaded into the activity of writing poetry—during the period between his review of Lowell's *Near the Ocean* in 1967 and the *Sewanee Review* essay titled "The Act of Love: Poetry and Personality" published about a decade later. He uses the term "personality," by his own admission, very nearly as it was used by Nicolas Berdyaev, though without Berdyaev's Christian application, to mean the whole individual subjectivity, spirit and body and soul as a bundled indivisibility of being. Personality, in Carruth's words, "is a phenomenon of pure existence and occurs in what have been called existential moments," instants outside time, untouched by the determinations of history, biology, society. The freedom he describes, and insists on, is the freedom of subjectivity struggling to express its presence as archetype. This assertion strikes against the grain of much of the criticism taught and practiced these days in universities, where all poems are thought reducible to their ideological or social determinants, and that "existential moments" are yet another intellectual fiction contrived by ideology. In the essay, published in 1976, Carruth himself lamented what he saw to be a failure of authenticity, a miscarriage of personality in some of the poetry then being written and praised. He saw personality practiced as solipsism. "Instead of responsibility to life," he wrote, "instead of responsibility to his own personality as archetype of life, the poet now is responsible to his own personality and nothing more." The abridgement of the existentialist ethic Carruth found in Berdyaev had led finally to a perhaps unavoidable "license to indulge the self."

I read the essay some years after it appeared. I had in the meantime formed my own opinions about personality, partly in reaction to the kind of poetry that commanded so much attention in the mid- and late-1970's, but mostly to help me find my way when I was writing poetry. I believed that personality as existentialist process had been so trivialized that it was reduced to a theatrical configuration of selfhood contrived for rhetorical effect. It seemed to me—and what now seems to me a little blustery and supercilious I then experienced very clearly as a lifeline to what I considered important in poetry—that personality had become a cult object and that as such it enfeebled poetry's capacity to gather up the world and its imaginations. The cult of personality had displaced simple self-interrogating moral presence. Casual preciosities of perception were valued over impassioned deliberation. Maybe this is still evident in our poetry; maybe it is always apparent in approved, middlebrow styles. At any rate, what I detested was the coquettish, self-protective objectification of personality. To clarify things, over against personality I set experience, the encounter with all that is not the subject, not the "me." While I believed that the intensest subjectivity was the essence of lyric poetry, I wanted a subjectivity so fused to experience that the two could not be told apart. It was a fairly puritanical view, and at the time I was under the sway of Perry Miller's extraordinary book on Jonathan Edwards. I did not then see that my position was too defensive, and that setting off personality against experience was too much an intellectual convenience which finally hardened both and took them too much out of the turbulence and changefulness of life.

    The crucial term in Carruth's remarks is transcendence. As he pursues his argument in that essay, he tells us that personality is a "dynamic process, a process of transcendence, extending always beyond oneself." This pulls us out of any conception we might have of personality as something static, a willed exaltation of idiosyncrasy. He situates the issue in its proper place, in our world of constantly mixed and revised orders. He admits to some perplexity about the end or destination, what he calls the "*toward-which*," of transcendence, though late in the essay he speculates that the direction of that movement of the soul "is for each consciousness in its own personality to answer, and the answer will be in its own terms." Subjectivity, personality, is essentially action, and it is the action of seeking something away from or other than its own articulated self. There's no need, therefore, to escape from personality, only from the crass or mercantile or debilitating solipsism that personality may lead to. Personality is not a condition, it is a way, a passage. Moreover, Carruth believes it is a passage of inwardness. If personality and the urge for transcendence direct us *away*, as he says, it directs us *away toward* the interior, the mysterious center: "Transcendence is a pushing through the petals of memory and feeling toward the deeper center of the flower."

His poetry has been the story of his own seeking. His has been a genuine self-interrogating moral presence, though that is my term and he may cringe to hear it said of him, so wary he has always been of any suggestion of pieties of any sort. The crucial act in the process of seeking, he says in his essay, is love, "spiritual love, the state of being of a pure existence, and the aesthetic emotion is the experience of that state." For me, the purest expression of it is "This Song" in *From Snow and Rock, From Chaos*. It's a poem that gathers in its telling observations from a walk in the fields of northern Vermont in early fall and makes that gathering an articulation of the journey of subjectivity—or one stage of it, at least—of personality seeking transcendence through eros. He walks not only in a time of day, in an afternoon "bright with September," but also in a spirit-time, in "an old dissension/bright with fear." He sees and notes (with that superb, casual, intense countryman's eye of his) the lively variety of field flowers; he also sees how ferns "taken by frost,/made russet the fields and turned/the waysides yellow and brown." His spirit life bleeds into the fall tones of the landscape; he realizes that he has wandered nearly all his life in this way, and that the object of the long search is "the touch that heals" and the "look that says *I know*." But there is no touch, and no such look. The long Vermont winter is coming, and at its threshold—one of the many that have been and are to come—Carruth still seeks what he knows does not wait for him. The beautiful last stanza tells us what he finds:

> I feel September's little knives, and with my eyes
> I see bright spattered leaves in the matted
> grass. I hear this song, if it be a song: these
> insistent little bright fearful hesitant
> murmurs from high in the old pine trees.

What is this transcendence? I believe it is the pain and desire of the way of subjectivity he describes in his essay. In his own terms, "This Song" is the clearest of love songs, a cry of eros, of the craving and needfulness to find something other, once lost, that it may join and be healed, made finally sane and whole.

David Rivard

A Meaning of Hayden Carruth

Several seasons back in the age of post-capitalism, I was home one Friday night, watching a Celtics-Knicks game on television. Bored by the half-time interviews and recitation of stats, I started flipping channels, eventually coming to an episode of *Miami Vice* already well in progress. What caused me to stop was the sight and sound of a man in a wheelchair—heavyset, bearded, wild haired, Latin American, and dressed in the show's infamous pastel color scheme—rolling down the streets of Miami's "little Havana" barrio, careening drunkenly, while reciting, "An aging man is but a paltry thing,/A tattered coat upon a stick, unless/Soul clap its hands and sing, and louder sing...." The actor played the part of a famous national poet, a leftist in exile (from where didn't seem to concern the director), being shadowed by a death squad. Getting past the incongruity of hearing "Sailing To Byzantium" recited (and not too badly either) on the most popular television show in America, as well as the unintended political ironies created by the situation (Yeats, not Neruda?), I was struck by an equally unintended truth revealed in the portrayal—the myth of the great self, the poet as heroic personality, the personality as the poetry.

Maybe this episode of *Miami Vice* is simply just another example of the post-modernist ransacking of cultural and political history, part of the blurring of distinctions between high and "popular" arts. It's a convention of the age. But post-modernism, despite all its attacks on the Romantic "I," hasn't been totally successful at shaking the various notions of personality—all emphasizing, consciously or unconsciously, the importance of the self—inherited from the Romantics, filtered through the Modernists, and proliferating in unforeseen ways in later generations. The celebration of the heroic "I" and its isolating dramas, its sensitivities and anxieties, goes largely unquestioned. Worse, our culture, emphasizing as it does the primacy of "the individual," seems to promote a notion of self as consumable (and marketable) product. As Robert Hass, for one, has noted, "the establishment of distinctions of personality by peripheral means is just what consumer society is about." Poets, no less than the purchasers of Tony Lama boots, BMW's or lingerie from Victoria's Secret, are caught up in these cultural forces.

Personality, not person. One popular model of selfhood available to the contemporary poet is, to use Peter Stitt's phrase, "the sincerist." These lines from a poem by Edward Hirsch, with their metaphorically fashioned pose of the tormented poet as "prisoner," illustrate some of the inherent problems of personality-driven work:

> It hurts me to remember how I lived then,
> Desolate as my narrow room, roaming the streets
> Hour after hour
>   as if I were carrying out the terms
> Of a life-sentence,
>   condemned to search
> The blank, exhausted faces of passing strangers....
>   (from "Homage to O'Keeffe")

The struggle of the self with loneliness and despair feels puffed up here (ironically, it actually glorifies despair). It is framed by the presence of "Jackson's bridal shop," a morning "disc jockey" on the poet's alarm clock/radio, "the #23 bus," the "janitor" sawing in the basement—a package of items that suggest the poet's status as a plain-spoken, heroic Everyman. But does the poet truly connect with others through these details? No. He only *uses* them to confirm the veracity or "reality" of the self enacted by the poem, to achieve the feel of direct, untransformed reportage from the poet's life. Similarly, the poster of Georgia O'Keeffe's *Evening Star* on his "cell" wall strategically assures us of the poet's sensitivity, his unswerving belief in the redemptive powers of art. But the "sincerist" is not alone. At the opposite extreme, that of the so-called LANGUAGE poets, the version of self which likes to go by the name of "avantgarde" constructs itself. Charles Bernstein, one of the movement's leading theorists, starts a recent piece this way:

> Thanks for your of already some
> weeks ago. Things
> very much back to having returned
> to a life that

> (regrettably) has very little in
> common with, a
> totally bright few
> or something like
> it. Was
> delighted to get
> a most remarkable & am assuming
> all continues, well
> thereabouts. Fastens
> the way of which spiral
> fortuitously by leaps
> and potions, countering thingamajig
> whoseits.
>
> (from "The Age Of Correggio
> And The Carrachi")

This beginning, with its interrupted consciousness, seems to imply Bernstein's poem has little in common with Hirsch's—the speaker's voice is not reliable, its referents are undeterminable, it is militantly abstract, and it avoids detail or later in the poem presents it in a non-linear fashion. Yet, the two share a hunger to establish an identifiable persona. In Bernstein's case, it is that of the poet alienated from the tradition and mainstream, a "radical," a "pioneer," an "outlaw" of sorts, another version of the poet as hero. The language of the poem announces his resistance to the formulaic strategies, the conventions, of the "academic" workshop—what more Romantic assumption than to posit the individual or oppressed group in rebellion against an institution. Bernstein's belief (shared by the LANGUAGE poets) that words are non-referential, that they don't point to any existing emotion or object or idea, would seem to help undercut notions of the self as "consumable product." Yet, this belief, marked by a radical individuality of perception and creation, is simply another indulgence of the self. And the belief shapes expectations about the correct "form" of poems, expectations that are every bit as marketable as those of "sincereism" (just not as profitable).

It's probably unfair to single out these poets, when nearly all of us are afflicted by this disease. But, overwhelmingly, the body of contemporary American poetry proves one of Simone Weil's points about modern life, that its art is often no more than the mere expression of personality. On the other hand, says Weil,

> Gregorian chant, Romanesque architecture, the Iliad, the invention of geometry, were not, for the people through whom they were brought into being and made available to us, occasions for the manifestation of personality.

In his essay, "A Meaning of Robert Lowell," Hayden Carruth makes a point that reinforces Weil's. Carruth describes Lowell's defect as "the temptation to mere appearance, to effects, trappings—to the extraneous." The "I" in Lowell's poems (especially after *Life Studies*) rests on this impulse. This leads away, in the poems, from the creation of the sense of a whole being, what Carruth calls, in another essay, "the whole individual subjectivity, the spirit-body-soul." For Carruth, this subjectivity equates with neither individuality nor surface personality. It is based, not on an autobiographical "I," but on a displacement of self. This act of displacement should not imply any ignoring of the self, its sufferings and joys; rather, the self must become a kind of emblem of transformation, of the movement away from the solipsistic ego. It involves, as Allen Grossman has said, "speaking to history words other than those which history can speak." And it means acknowledging, as Carruth so often does, the great fluidity of self-identity, a dynamic process which is constantly and necessarily being altered by those we live among and those who have lived before us. The radical self-doubt evident throughout Carruth's work never undermines his sense of responsibility to life, to "other." In fact, it is the driving force behind his desire to create links to community. "The work of the poet," he says, "is self-transcendence."

In Carruth's view, Lowell's "too-great concentration of effort upon the verbal surface" (in *Near The Ocean* and other work) produces a distorted brilliance-for-brilliance-sake. He argues that these excesses of rhetoric, syntax and figurative language become Lowell's persona, his tone, his "meaning," and that they actually obscure the poet and his life (despite Lowell's allegiance to autobiography).

Although it feels exaggerated to me, paying only cursory attention to Lowell's often tremendous originality of vision, it's still a criticism with no small validity. In fact, sometimes the effect of Lowell's writing is unintentionally comic, as in this couplet from "No Hearing:" "I watch the muddy breakers bleach to beerfroth,/our steamer, THE STATE OF MAINE, an iceberg at drydock." In other instances, what seems inspired turns out to be merely confused, as in this description of a house:

> Tonight, though, I see it shine
> in the Azores of my open window.
> Its manly, old-fashioned lines
> are gorgeously rectilinear.
> It's like some firework to be fired
> at the end of the garden party,
> some Spanish *casa*, luminous
> with heraldry and murder,
> marooned in New York.
> (from "The Opposite House")

This passage moves, undeniably, with a wonderful economy and precision; yet, what does it add up to? A series of questions. Why is the view an "Azores"? How exactly is the building "like some firework"? And why does it shift shape to become the *"casa"*? The context provided by the poem offers no answers. While aiming at imaginative objective description, perhaps these figures only really define the speaker's state of mind, or the mind as personality. And even the great bravery and technical accomplishment of Lowell's best work is sometimes undermined by an isolating self-drama, one which goes unresisted: "I hear/my ill-spirit sob in each blood cell,/as if my hand were at its throat.... /I myself am hell;/nobody's here...." Lowell's illness was very real, his struggles with it often deeply moving, but a passage like this offers us only a steel cage disguised as a confrontation with the self.

Carruth's poetry has largely avoided the emphasis on an apparently direct and unmediated autobiography, the creation of a recognizable persona, all the while undermining the notion of hyper-sensitivity as heroic. In "Simple," for example, a poem which ritualizes the memory of a separation and loss in quatrains composed of varying 2–3 beat lines, he gives shape through myth-making to the experience of madness:

> how we made a pier, a jetty
>   of lights, a brightness
> in that fantastic dark,
>   down which we took our way
>
> to the vessel that lay in the
>   shadows....

The pier and jetty lights seem to echo an image which occurs in a passage of *The Bloomingdale Papers,* Carruth's book of poems written thirty years earlier and detailing his institutionalization for psychiatric disorders. There, he remembers sitting "at the end of the long curving jetty/whose base is attached to the city of Chicago." Here the place becomes one of leave-taking from an unknown person. After which, Carruth says, "... I turned/back into the knowledge of going/crazy from loneliness." But the poem doesn't want simply to follow his descent into illness; there's a resistance to the potential bathos of the situation, and that resistance feeds itself on *imagination.* "Looking/back," he writes, "I imagine":

> how I retired to a room
>   I built, perhaps
>
> a kiva lit by reflections
>   of the moon, where I
> celebrated over and over
>   the trembling mysteries
>
> of loss. I became a living
>   brain in an effigy
> of reeds and cloth and paint,
>   completely insane.

The drama of the self is deflected into an imagined space, quite literally here a room that becomes a kiva, a structure used by the Pueblo Indians for ceremonies, often underground. Against the self-destructive tendencies of the mind ("a living/brain in an effigy/of reeds and cloth and paint") he pits the freedom of the self to create, to transform and redeem the experience of feeling oneself made nothing by madness. The space of the poem, the poem as a "kiva," allows him this freedom. The architecture of the final stanza, with its pattern of slant end-rhyme and its perfectly iambic penultimate line, clearly argues for it. Just as the words themselves argue not for an ennobling of madness, or a self-pity, but for a kind of sorrowful wonder at it after all this time.

If one thinks of Robert Lowell's poems about his own institutionalizations, the contrast is immediate and instructive. For example, the ending and especially the final couplet of Lowell's "Waking in the Blue" ("We are all old timers,/each of us holds a locked razor"), seems, ultimately, stagy or postured, its ironic realism a merely aesthetic resolution—neither as terrifying as the "effigy" made in Carruth's poem, nor as absolutely and understatedly factual as his final line's "completely insane." Instead, Carruth's poem has a freshness to it, a liveliness of music inseparable from vision, part of its refusal to romanticize suffering.

This feel of music is what Carruth calls "spontaneous improvisation within a fixed and simple form," the heart of jazz, one of his great influences. Improvisation, as a value, might be opposed to the artifice and "shapedness" seen in Lowell, the emphasis on aesthetic product. In an essay titled, "Some Influences: The Formal Idea of Jazz," he makes this proposal:

> What happens, subjectively and spiritually, when a musician improvises freely? He transcends the objective world, including the objectively conditioned ego, and becomes a free, undetermined sensibility in communion with others....

Communion. This is what marks the difference between Carruth and Lowell. A life, Carruth writes, is created by "a series of successive imaginative acts." For him, this power can only be fulfilled through a responsibility to others. In his essay on Lowell, he comes at the issue by claiming that self-creation must move outside the self, toward the other, for the reader's sake. Otherwise it is of no use, it concocts a stick-figure, mere personality; and, as in the case of Lowell, it may lead to the evolving of a style "too much like a shell, a carapace, and extraneity."

For Carruth, improvisation is achieved through "the disciplines of the instrumental imagination." Metaphor is one of these disciplines. In his poems it is largely a way to get at our essential relatedness, an entrance into, as he says in "The Ravine," "the relationship between things." That poem recognizes and weaves such relationships:

> Stone, brown tufted grass, but no water,
> it is dry to the bottom. A seedy eye
> of orange hawkweed blinks in sunlight
> stupidly, a mink bumbles away,
> a ringnecked snake among stones lifts its head
> like a spark, a dead young woodcock —
> long dead, the mink will not touch it —
> sprawls in the hatchment of its soft plumage
> and clutches emptiness with drawn talons.
> This is the ravine today. But in spring it
> cascaded, in winter it filled with snow
> until it lay hidden completely. In time,
> geologic time, it will melt away
> or deepen beyond recognition, a huge
> gorge. These are what I remember and foresee.
> These are what I see here every day,
> not things but relationships of things,
> quick changes and slow. These are my sorrow,
> for unlike my bright admonitory friends
> I see relationships, I do not see things.
> These, such as they are, every day, every
> unique day, the first in time and the last,
> are my thoughts, the sequences of my mind.
> I wonder what they mean. Every day,
> day after day, I wonder what they mean.

There are many wonderful things about this poem. The hawkweed blinking "stupidly," the mink that "bumbles" away (verb and adverb perhaps also describing the speaker's mind?) — brief moments of comedy in the landscape that give way to the horror of the dead woodcock. The woodcock, which becomes a Zen-like emblem both of non-fulfillment and courage. The contradiction of starting this poem about "relationships," about process, with a beautifully rendered catalog of things. And the more meditative passage that follows it, reminding me a little of Stevens, the Stevens, say, of "Esthetique du Mal"–a music of grave, pivoting phrases running inside the lineaments of argument, the construct of avowal, repetition, and conjunction. The music itself seeking to replicate the feel of relationship as an activity in which one partakes, and outside of which one also remains.

But what I love about "The Ravine" is the leap Carruth takes toward the end: "These ... are my thoughts, the sequences of my mind." With a precise ambiguity, "these" is made to refer back to "relationships," and the mind–the self here–is metaphorically transformed into the process it has been describing. All distance collapses in the speaker's identification, "every/unique day, the first in time and the last." For Carruth, this is a sort of *ars poetica*. The more so because its final two lines, characteristically, blend together curiosity, humility, awe, horror, and acceptance.

In an essay called "Found In Translation: On A Social History of The Moral Imagination," the anthropologist Clifford Geertz describes one condition of mind and its process of imaginatively giving shape to the world in a way similar to Carruth in "The Ravine." Referring to Faulkner, he points to

> how what happens, recountings of what happens, and metaphoric transfigurations of recountings of what happens into general visions, pile, one on top of the next, to produce a state of mind at once more knowing, more uncertain, and more disequilibriated.

A state which makes, as in Carruth's case, for an openness toward life, for an essential inquisitiveness–a hunger for connection.

The voice of Carruth's poetry is always aware of its relatedness, of community, of sympathy. Much of the time, it has been a poetry of people in specific locales: the rural scene in particular, the life of small farms in the Vermont hills–one of difficult, constant work–and other places, upstate New York, the small city turned fast-food strip and mall, the psychiatric hospital, small-town

Connecticut, as well as remote stretches of history. He has written of these places with the wisdom and humor and horror that belong to their people, and especially to his family and friends. Not only their lives, but their very voices have been brought into his work. And he has done the same with nature, so that we see ourselves as one species among many.

It's easy to feel Carruth's spontaneity, his inquiring empathy, as a form of wonder, as what makes even the most despairing of his poems seem vibrant. It is probably the reason why many of his best poems are about work, especially farm work, where communal relations, the necessity of helping others, the interdependence of lives, are always a felt presence, as strong as the natural landscape.

Empathy locates itself in what we most have in common. If work is one, suffering is another. And the two often coincide in Carruth's poetry, as in "Emergency Haying." At the opening of this poem, the descriptive plainness of riding home on a wagon, exhausted and cut-up after haying all day, gives way to a crucifixion image, not an identification with the suffering of Christ but a sympathy with it (a risky distinction, which I think he pulls off by undercutting it slightly with the ironic aside: "Well, I change grip and the image/fades.") "It's been an unlucky summer," he writes, and the brief catalog of difficulties that follows is as trenchantly and plainly stated as the explanation it ends with: "and Marshall needs help."

> We mow, rake, bale and draw the bales
> to the barn, these late, half-green,
> improperly cured bales: some weigh 100 pounds
>
> or more, yet must be lugged by the twine
> across the field, tossed on the load, and then
> at the barn unloaded on the conveyor
>
> and distributed in the loft. I help—
> I, the desk-servant, word-worker
> and hold up my end pretty well too; but God,
>
> the close of day, how I fall down then. My hands
> are sore, they flinch when I light my pipe.
> I think of those who have done slave labor,
>
> less able and less well-prepared than I.

In the meditation on oppression and torture that follows, Carruth is careful not to appropriate that suffering or to glorify it for his own sake. It's why, in the passage I just quoted, he is honest enough to see himself as both different from and the same as Marshall, as "the desk-servant, word-worker." The distinction is real and necessary; though I love the way it and the loose pentameter of the poem is cut against by the colloquial assertion, "I help ... and hold up my end pretty well too."

When Carruth emerges from his cataloging of "clerks and housekeepers/herded to the gaunt fields of torture," he looks around to the surrounding hills, the trees just coming into fall color. And it feels as if the inspiration of the New England landscape (an inspiration come to a little ironically: "I look beyond/our famous hayfields to our famous hills"), the movement into it, is what takes him to the uprising—and another kind of acknowledgement of Christ—which ends the poem:

> .... It must be so. My strength
> is legion. And I stand up high
> on the wagon tongue in my whole bones to say
>
> woe to you, watch out
> you sons of bitches who would drive men and women
> to the fields where they can only die.

Though it feels self-conscious, and intentionally inflated in its gesture, the pentameter breaking down in the anger, its effort and passage out of the self moves me.

Marshall, the neighbor Carruth mentions in "Emergency Haying," is the subject of one of the remarkable series of character studies and dramatic monologues published in *Brothers, I Loved You All* (as well as in *If You Call This Cry a Song* and *Asphalt Georgics*). "Marshall Washer" is an essay/meditation, through the character of Marshall, on the life of farms in northern New England and on the nature of friendship. Moving, in sections, from the general and archetypal to the particular and personal, Carruth's aim doesn't seem so much the realistic delineation of character or psychology as the rendering of a moral sensibility: "the remnant of human worth/to admire in this world, and I think to envy." The idea of fate figures strongly in this poem, as well as in the others like it. They are a little reminiscent of Robinson in this, or of Frost (the locale is familiar enough, so is the colloquial blank verse). But there's little of the distance, the view from tragic heights, that one feels in either Frost or Robinson. Carruth's sympathetic nature probably wouldn't allow it.

In the strongest (and most terrifying) of these pieces, "Marvin McCabe," it is this sympathy which allows him to create a character who is, unlike Marshall Washer, a figure for the situation of the poet's self. In attempting to speak for McCabe (who is unable to talk due to an auto accident), Carruth enacts the fundamental problem of the poet: how to speak for other lives. In McCabe's nihilism you can feel Carruth questioning his own assumptions about the possibility of transcendence and meaning. The poem is almost a kind of extended metaphor, constructed to test his feeling (articulated in his essay on Berdyaev's *Slavery and Freedom*) that in our time "we seem to have come to a point where the poet is utterly lost in himself." Initially, he sets up this test by laying out the conditions of McCabe's life – the cruel father who is a rural laborer, escape into alcohol and cars, the pregnant girlfriend, and war service – until he arrives at the auto accident that robs McCabe, the speaker of this interior monologue, of his motor functions, most seriously of speech. "The usual story here in the mountains," says Carruth through McCabe. It has more than a touch of melodrama, or would if it weren't undercut by the weird and homely humor present in McCabe's voice:

> ... The talk machine's busted,
> that's all. Connections all screwed up. Have you ever
> wondered how it would be to have your thought
> that's clear and shiny inside your head come out
> like a mouthful of mud? As for simple things,
> I say, "Ahwan ahg' abah' "– what does it mean?
> I say it five times, "Ahwan ahg' abah',"
> grimacing and smiling, *pleading,* and no one
> hears me say I want to go to the bathroom.
> I have to take a leak, for Christ's sake!

Or, this, a little later:

> ... What
> I'm thinking now—and most of the time—is how
> I wish whoever invented beer had been stuffed
> back and smothered in his mother's womb.

What would it be like to lose the ability to talk, and how possible is it, really, to speak for someone else? Or for ourselves, for that matter. The joke, it turns out, is on all of us. The speaker gestures toward Carruth, who "knows not only what I'm saying but what/I mean to say...." But even that acknowledgement is over-ridden late in the poem:

> ... But the hardest
> of all was always this feeling that my thoughts
> were shut inside me, that all I could *do* was smile.
> I knew the words but couldn't say them—do you
> know what that means? *No one knew who I was.*
> It was like those people who believe your soul
> can pass into another body when you die.
> I was in the wrong body, but I hadn't died.
> Can jail be worse than that? I wanted to die.
> I would have if wanting could do it. But then
> I came to see it doesn't make any difference.
> If I spoke, what would it do?—my thoughts mean nothing,
> my life means nothing, my death means nothing.
> And everything means nothing.

It has an appalling and blasted feel, this passage. It reminds me, too, of the somewhat more gentle ending of one of Randall Jarrell's best poems, "Next Day," another persona poem:

> How young I seem; I *am* exceptional;
> I think of all I have.
> But really no one is exceptional,
> No one has anything, I'm anybody,
> I stand beside my grave
> Confused with my life, that is commonplace and solitary.

The Rilkean undertones of Jarrell's writing, the mention of the "grave" with the communal associations and consolation of the burial ceremony, tend to mitigate the message in ways that are impossible in "Marvin McCabe." In Carruth's poem, we witness an understanding that collapses into existential nothingness. But, paradoxically, when that nothingness is taken inside, it levels all boundaries between self and other. It's no real consolation, except that it teaches us a bravery which we didn't know we were capable of, the bravery of our humanness:

> ... This body is wrong, a misery,
> a misrepresentation, but hell, would talking make
> any difference? The reason nobody knows me
> is because I don't exist. And neither do you.

I think it is as frightening an epiphany as I know of in the poetry of the last thirty years, made only more so by the sly jocularity of "a misrepresentation." But its courage and severe lucidity feel like a challenge—by Carruth, to himself and to us—a dare to make meaning out of meaninglessness. And it is more compelling for having been rendered in the speech of the everyday.

The tragic finds its music in the everyday, common speech being only one form of it. Jazz—as I've already mentioned, one of Carruth's primary influences—is another, and it can move us beyond the tragic. The influence arises from his twinned need for "freedom and discipline," by which means he has "interfused thematic improvisation and ... metrical predictability." Jazz embodies his understanding of how, as he writes,

> in its moments of transcendent freedom the self is, in fact, a
> communion with the other, though how to define that other still
> escapes me. I think it may be the transcendent selves of all
> human imaginations not irreparably maimed by the life of machines
> in the objective world. I call it love.
> (Introduction to *Effluences
> from the Sacred Caves*)

In a poem like "Bears at Raspberry Time" this aspect of love is visible in the way in which the self is not quite speaking for itself but being spoken for by the life that surrounds it. This is the beginning of the poem:

Fear. Three bears
are not fear, mother
and cubs come berrying
in our neighborhood

like any other family.
I want to see them, or any
distraction. Flashlight
poking across the brook

in briary darkness,
but they have gone,
noisily. I go to bed.
Fear. Unwritten books

already titled. Some
idiot will shoot the bears
soon, it always happens,
they'll be strung up by the paws

in someone's frontyard
maple to be admired and
measured, and I'll be paid
for work yet to be done —

with a broken imagination.

An effect similar to call-and-response sets itself up here, in the shuttling back and forth between the speaker's woes and the bears, in the torsion between the sentence fragments and shorter clauses and phrasings and the unwinding of the longer sentences. You catch the feel of it too in the fourth and fifth stanzas, in the movement from "some" to "soon," which is echoed at "strung" and "someone," then slurs down to "done" and "imagination." This is song as a tracking through consciousness. "Is middle age what makes/even dreams factual?" asks Carruth. The answer comes in the return of the bears later in the evening. That is, the bears *seem* to come back, he can't "be sure." But the wish for their presence is a mark of Carruth's affection for them, for life, and it carries him beyond the repetitions of "fear."

Carrying the motion outward: the transmission of energy, located in love. In "Sometimes When Lovers Lie Quietly Together, Unexpectedly One of Them Will Feel The Other's Pulse" (a somewhat comically prolix title), from *Lighter Than Air Craft*, Carruth finds the pulse of the two lovers quite literally in a pair of power lines swinging rhythmically in noonday sun:

> Above the street at heavy opalescent noontime two electrical
>   cables, strung from pole to pole,
> Hung in relationship to one another such that the lower
>   swung in and out of the shadow of the one above it,
> And as it did so the sunlight reflected from it was sprung
>   gleaming outward and inward along its length,
> A steady expansion and contraction. And for a while I was
>   taken away from my discontents
> By this rhythm of the truth of the world, so fundamental, so
>   simple, so clear.

The unfolding of syntax hugs the visual in these long lines—lines probably more influenced by Ovid than Whitman. It comes to rest, wonderfully lulled, in his being "taken away from my discontents/ By this rhythm of the truth of the world." I think this rootedness in love, and the way love is carried into the world, is what has always moved me in Carruth's work. Even though it is the habit of the self to turn away and in, even though, as he says in section 9 of the long poem "Paragraphics," it was his "custom" to "be silent,/ to think the song inwardly":

> Yet sometimes two
> heard it, two separately together. It could come
> nearby in the shadow of a pine bough
> on the snow, or high in the orchestral lights,
> or maybe (this was our miracle) it would have no
> intermediary—
>   a suddenness,
>   indivisible, unvoiced.

This "suddenness" is the singing of transcendence. It rests on the deepest understanding of how, in Simone Weil's words, "shifting fortune and necessity hold in subject every human spirit...." Yet, the possibility of achieving this understanding is, as she wrote, "fraught with temptations to falsehood, temptations that are positively enhanced by pride, by shame, by hatred, contempt, indifference, by the will to oblivion or ignorance." These are the temptations that Hayden Carruth has sung himself past. And for taking us with him, I'm grateful.

Maxine Kumin

On "North Winter"

Early Carruth, "North Winter" was first published by The Prairie Press of Iowa City in 1963 and reprinted in *For You*, brought out by New Directions in 1970. Since it is wholly omitted from *The Selected Poetry*, which Macmillan published in 1985—a reasonable decision, as it would not excerpt well— it seems especially fitting to discuss it here.

"North Winter" is a tone poem in 57 strophes, subtly modulated here and there with little skips and riffs of typographical invention. Not "concrete" poetry, but lightly shaped, like a homemade loaf.

In one instance, a stanza is playfully elongated perhaps to resemble its subject, a white birch tree in which five blue jays perch, discussing "goodandevil." In another, a rather more ambitious shaping seems to imitate the letter Z. The subject is "the wintering mountain"; the shape is suggestive of the gradual transformation evoked by falling snow. I read wit and humor into this concoction, along with a stringent desire to be accurate, apt and vivid. One last example, again involving snow: Carruth is keenly observant. He is a watcher of snow falling. Who could have said it more succinctly than with this modelling?

"Snow's downstrokes climb softly up the c $o^{n^{i}f}e_{r}$."

The language ranges from direct declarative—"The brook has holes in its cover/this morning"— to an almost pervid anthropomorphism in which "new deer tracks" tell "of revels by night/of joy and delight and happiness/beyond any power of consciousness" and "The tamarack with needles lost/and a thousand curled-up twigs/like dead birdsfeet takes/the snow greedily and in snatches/to cover its misshapen nakedness." But this exuberant romanticism which teeters on the rim of pathetic fallacy is checked and balanced elsewhere by Carruth's gift for clean, accurate observation, as in #21:

> The spaniel flies with his ears
> across the snow carrying a
> deer's legbone in his jaws

> the bone flops threejointedly
> and the little hoof dances
> delicately in the snow.

And again, #52:

> Small things
>   hardest to believe
> redpoll snatching
>   drops from an icicle.

This precision requires great control, a kind of compression of language against which Carruth rebels, as it were, with occasional bursts of exuberance. Could John Berryman have read this excerpt? The voice is not far from Henry's.

> death knowledge being heady
> it hath not the beasts' beauty
> goeth tricksy and ploddy
> and usually too damn wordy
> but drunken or topsyturvy
> gladhanding tea'd or groovy
> it arriveth
> it arriveth
> o you pretty lady

Carruth is attracted to unusual words, sometimes archaic, sometimes technical, as in "sneaping winds" and "the frazil flux of identities." *Sneaping* sounds like its denotation, nipping or pinching, but *frazil*, a term used for anchor ice—ice formed at the bottom of a stream—is harder to come by. Describing an old cellarhole in the woods, Carruth speaks of "the gravamen of old stones," carrying us back beyond the technical legal meaning of the word to its origin in late Latin, where it denoted a weighing down, a burden.

He invents, too. Describing the sounds of crossbills scissoring open seeds, he calls them "a fidget for ears *enpomped* in the meadow's silence," evoking for me a procession of small furry ears alertly turned. The word has a wonderful texture; we can allow meanings to ray out from it.

A master of exactitude, Carruth catches the essential glassiness implicit in *vitrescent* snowcrust, the nausea behind the weaving gait in *wamble*, the wild progression of numbers rising up to a billion in *milliard*, in British usage the cardinal number represented by 1 followed by 9 zeros.

The poet as namer: redpoll and crossbill, his winter birds. Dogtooth, anemone, arbutus, his earliest flowers. Birches, beeches, balsams, scotch pines, spruces, maples, his eternal trees. Ice and icicle, degrees Fahrenheit, snow in a dozen configurations. To name is to possess. As Rilke put it in the ninth Duino elegy:

> Maybe we're here only to say: *house,*
> *bridge, well, gate, jug, olive tree, window* —
> at most, *pillar, tower* ... but to say them, remember,
> oh, to say them in a way that the things themselves
> never dreamed of existing so intensely.

I cherish this plain statement (and indeed drew on it for a book title of my own). For to be a poet is to take possession not of material things but of the numinous aspects of the world around us. I write this sentence as winter descends on New England, the first steady snowfall of the season —"the judaskisses of snow"— having its noiseless way.

"North Winter" is a poem to cherish, made up of small truths that run from first snow through bittersweet cold to spring thaw. Like Thoreau's *Walden*, it bears up well under annual reading, yielding each time a new pleasure.

David Weiss

Taking Sides

Out of context, it might seem a comic moment: the picture of a man "lank with sweat" at the close of day standing on the tongue of a hay wagon piled high with bales, calling out, "woe to you, watch out/you sons of bitches who would drive men and women/to the fields where they can only die." Comic because ludicrous: who can hear him over the roar of the tractor in his rural remoteness? Comic because hopeless even if he were heard: who would take his admonition seriously? Comic, too, because ridiculous: who speaks this way except prophets and madmen? "Woe to you" is a phrase pitched inversely to its helplessness and indignation, the speaker of it resembling the little tramp in Chaplin's "Modern Times." This is the way Hayden Carruth's "Emergency Haying" ends. Since I will speak about it for most of this essay, here is the entire poem:

> Coming home with the last load I ride standing
> on the wagon tongue, behind the tractor
> in hot exhaust, lank with sweat,
>
> my arms strung
> awkwardly along the hayrack, cruciform.
> Almost 500 bales we've put up
>
> this afternoon, Marshall and I.
> And of course I think of another who hung
> like this on another cross. My hands are torn
>
> by baling twine, not nails, and my side is pierced
> by my ulcer, not a lance. The acid in my throat
> is only hayseed. Yet exhaustion and the way
>
> my body hangs from twisted shoulders, suspended
> on two points of pain in the rising
> monoxide, recall that greater suffering.
>
> Well, I change my grip and the image
> fades. It's been an unlucky summer. Heavy rains
> brought on the grass tremendously, a monster crop,
>
> but wet, always wet. Haying was long delayed.
> Now is our last chance to bring in
> the winter's feed, and Marshall needs help.

We mow, rake, bale, and draw the bales
to the barn, these late, half-green,
improperly cured bales; some weigh 100 pounds

or more, yet must be lugged by the twine
across the field, tossed on the load, and then
at the barn unloaded on the conveyor

and distributed in the loft. I help —
I, the desk-servant, word-worker —
and hold up my end pretty well too; but God,

the close of day, how I fall down then. My hands
are sore, they flinch when I light my pipe.
I think of those who have done slave labor,

less able and less well prepared than I.
Rose Marie in the rye fields of Saxony,
her father in the camps of Moldavia

and the Crimea, all clerks and housekeepers
herded to the gaunt fields of torture. Hands
too bloodied cannot bear

even the touch of air, even
the touch of love. I have a friend
whose grandmother cut cane with a machete

and cut and cut, until one day
she snicked her hand off and took it
and threw it grandly at the sky. Now

in September our New England mountains
under a clear sky for which we're thankful at last
begin to glow, maples, beeches, birches

in their first color. I look
beyond our famous hayfields to our famous hills,
to the notch where the sunset is beginning,

then in the other direction, eastward,
where a full new-risen moon like a pale
medallion hangs in a lavender cloud

beyond the barn. My eyes
sting with sweat and loveliness. And who
is the Christ now, who

> if not I? It must be so. My strength
> is legion. And I stand up high
> on the wagon tongue in my whole bones to say
>
> woe to you, watch out
> you sons of bitches who would drive men and women
> to the fields where they can only die.

In context, the absurdities I've described only hover, although necessarily, around its edges. The poet who writes these words is not unaware how nearly hollow and inadequate they sound. Only in a few poets—Pound, Wright, Duncan, Goodman, Berryman, for instance—does one find an equivalent reach for diction commensurate with the anguish of a feeling. Whether these final words ring true has a great deal to do with what this poem is about—the difference between life-sustaining and life-diminishing labor; between simile and metaphor; between relations illegitimate and true. Reviving a phrase like "woe to you" beyond a self-conscious or mannered use is part of the larger political impulse of the poem. To reclaim it is to reclaim right relations among people, to exert an influence. For what gets lost with the archaism of the phrase is its register of feeling. With its going, something in us goes too, or goes dormant. The poem works to restore its value. In this sense, of course, is a poet deeply conservative. He is on the side of what is lost, suppressed, obsolete, bypassed, unrealized; this affiliation is not utopic but Blakean—a rage at the toll taken on the human. His expression of rage requires a voice whose authority will be undeterred by the little it can do, although pained from the start that what is permitted is only a gesture, some words, "woe to you, watch out," a threat.

It is characteristic of Carruth, confronted with the fact of atrocity or injustice, not to be content with wounded sadness or resignation. Hatred, loathing, indignation are perhaps the hardest sentiments to get into poetry. We feel that they tend to turn a poem thin, shrill or judgmental. Their recalcitrance to poetry may say something, however, about the means by which certain moral responses can be voiced in verse. Carruth manages these feelings remarkably in "Adolf Eichmann."

>   and I say let the dung
> Be heaped on that man until it chokes his voice,
>
> Let him be made leprous so that the dung
> May snuggle to his bone, let his eyes be shut
> With slow blinding, let him be fed his own dung,
>
> But let his ears never, never be shut,
> And let young voices read to him, name by name,
> From the rolls of all those people whom he has shut
>
> Into the horrible beds, and let his name
> Forever and ever be the word for hate,
> Eichmann, cast out of the race, a loathsome name.

Here an infernal and straitened terza rima holds in check the poet's feeling. He is struggling with his own murderous emotions engendered by a greater hatred, but a like hatred nonetheless: "Lord, forgive me, I cannot keep down my hate."

The form provides the precedent for punishment; the decreating, Genesis-like imperatives provide its voice. In "Emergency Haying," the syntax of Carruth's indignation and the passing of judgement derive from Christ's warning to the Pharisees, those privileged ones. Its suprapersonal diction, paradoxically, allows him his fullest expression of feeling when the words are least his own. This understanding that one's voice and words are both one's own and others or, better put, individual and shared, is complicit with the poem's situation — the poet is helping his neighbor bale hay; if he doesn't lend a hand, the hay will be lost. There is probably no thought of not helping. He and his neighbor, as the poem "Marshall Washer" makes clear, are bound by a host of reciprocal arrangements and interlocking needs; they share, when necessary, tools, equipment, knowledge and labor. This idea of neighborliness, of voluntary but necessary association, is very much like the transhistorical relation to prior poets and poetry that Carruth and many poets have. It might even serve as a model for the way a poet belongs to the historical community of poets — borrowing, when in need, form, style, inspiration or precedent, and in turn sustaining that community by translation, allusion, indebtedness. A poet's self is an amalgam, then, and may depend on the number of, and extent to which, other, earlier poets are felt to be his true contemporaries. Neighborliness is not a gentle or genteel term; it is a fierce one and probably thrives in conditions which require it for survival.

Neighbors are united by their troubles, which make equals of them. This, importantly, is also what "Emergency Haying" is about. The poem's work is to expand its relation to others. It begins with one neighbor and ends up speaking for a supra-geographical neighborhood. This widening of relations is embedded in the word "woe." Its polysemy keeps the poet's anger from oversimplifying his poem. "Woe" also means sorrow or suffering and so, "woe to you" expresses a wish to transfer suffering to those who would cause it, yet not simply as punishment, but as a means of creating human ties, or their basis. Suffering is to a non-community what trouble is to a neighborly one: it can break down difference and forge, if momentarily, a commonality; to make those who inflict suffering suffer is, for Carruth, to bring an end to the endlessness of dehumanization, which we might define as a failure or inability to see others as like oneself and to feel what they feel. It may be that we must feel others to be fully human before we ourselves can be.

It is this empathetic act which Carruth takes as the essential function of metaphor. Early in "Emergency Haying" he rejects at first his likeness to Christ when it is based solely on his own pain and bodily position,

> And of course I think of another who hung
> like this on another cross. My hands are torn
>
> by baling twine, not nails, and my side is pierced
> by my ulcer, not a lance.........
> ....
>
> Well, I change my grip and the image
> fades.

Only after he recalls the forced and slave labor of others, and recalls their pain against the beauty of the changing season, "my eyes stinging with sweat and loveliness," will he accept an identification with Christ, "And who/is the Christ now, who//if not I?" This Christ is not the figure on the cross, however, but the one who speaks for the poor and the maimed; as a consequence, he can himself speak for those driven "to the fields where they can only die."

Early in the Odyssey when Telemachus calls a town meeting to announce his intent to sail in search of word of his father, two eagles swoop down, "tearing cheeks and throats" among the assembled. Halitherses, "keenest among the old/at reading birdflight into accurate speech," comes forward to prophesy the meaning of the event: Odysseus, like these birds, will soon return to do likewise to the suitors. The meaning of the sign is given analogically, which is in keeping with the meaning of *metapherein* – to cross beyond. The seer crosses the boundary of the human by means of metaphor to gain access to what only the gods can know – fate, the future, or (if it's a bardic art like Homer's, "Sing in me, muse, and through me tell the story") the whole of the past. Metaphors, of course, work variously. They can be used to domesticate and in doing so draw the strange into the ken of the familiar. They can appropriate and colonize by seeing things as other than they are, by turning them into something else. Carruth is sparing in these uses of metaphor, but he frequently engages in the act of crossing beyond. He does this in a number of ways; by taking on another's voice (as in "Marvin McCabe," one of the "legion"), or the voice of a place (as in "John Dryden"), or by adopting different genres and styles (like that manic mock-epic "A Little Old Funky Homeric Blues for Herm"). A Carruth poem frequently takes the discursive form of a man thinking his way beyond himself. The "beyond" in metaphor's root meaning allies itself with the beyond of ecstasy – ek-stasis, standing outside of – which for Carruth is the condition to which poetry and jazz aspire and the state in which they transpire ("freedom and discipline concur/only in ecstasy"). In "Emergency Haying" this happens with "Who is the Christ now, who//if not I?" One can glimpse from this that Carruth's aesthetics are a moral aesthetics whose transcendent aim must, to succeed, transform the world.

To go beyond oneself involves a loss of self or an enlargement of it. It can permit one to speak for another; yet it also can permit one to be spoken for. We occasionally feel this when we are reading. For a poet it can occur by slipping on the wordskins of another poet, as Carruth does in the song to his young son with which "A Little Fire in the Woods" closes: "Sweet Bo I know thee/thou art ten/and knowest now thy father is/fives times more again." It recalls Blake's "Little lamb who made thee?/Dost thou know who made thee?" Lines further on in Carruth's song, "the good firelight/is dying/the woods are sighing/and great is the dark," recall lines from another of the Poems of Innocence, "The Echoing Green": "Like birds in their nest,/Are ready to rest:/And sport no more seen/On the darkening Green." In this manner, Carruth puts on Blake's gentleness to laminate together succor, fragility, rightness, sorrow and instruction. I'd call this a neighborly enlargement, although Carruth has excoriated himself for "lacking a true voice,"

> What true voice? Where? Humiliated, in throes
> of vacillation, roundhead to cavalier to ivy league to
> smartass—
> never who I was.
> (from "Paragraphs")

There is some truth to this in his earlier poems. But a better way to see Carruth's use of neologisms, archaisms, borrowed diction and syntax is to notice that they appear at moments of "a little crisis," as he says, where a linguistic counterpressure is needed. "My strength is legion" and "woe to you" occur at such moments. This is a moment that often occurs in Wallace Stevens's poems where the balance of power between reality and imagination is at stake, where either "the world is ugly/and the people are sad" or "I was the world in which I walked and what I saw/Or heard or felt came not but from myself;/And there I found myself more truly and more strange." I bring Stevens in here because of the belief common to both poets that poetry is an agency of change in that continual confrontation of the self with the world. In Stevens, both extremes, imagination and reality, are unstable: both absence and excess of imagination are failures of imagination—failure to find the proper role of imagination—which the late poems overcome. "It was Ulysses and it was not," is how Stevens does it in "The World as Meditation." That "and" is a great one, comparable to the one which begins Pound's Cantos; it occupies the place of "The intensest rendezvous," where reality and imagination are not just Manichaean opposites, but complements. Nature's "inhuman meditation" which mends the trees—that is, Spring—is like Penelope's meditation on the sun as Ulysses; both are transformative. Imagination, here called "meditation" by Stevens, is the source of meaning and makes meaning without doing violence to reality, transforming without distorting "things as they are." Penelope's accomplishment is a victory of imagination over the self's own doubt.

I don't believe the confidence that Stevens expresses through Penelope is available to Carruth, or above suspicion—the world, for Carruth, is autonomously valuable and confers value; yet Carruth, too, is searching for "what will suffice." Nature's "inhuman meditation", Autumn's beauty and Carruth's meditation on human suffering clash. Carruth's meditation must include others. This is what drives "Emergency Haying." Yet something similar to "The World as Meditation" does take place, dynamically, in "Emergency Haying." The final stanzas balance authority and self-consciousness as if to say, "I am Christ and I am not." The conjunction, as in Stevens, allows both conditions to exist simultaneously. It perfectly marks the limits of the poet's power. It both rights the world and has no effect on it. It rights the world to the extent that Christ does—powerfully not at all. "Poetry makes nothing happen," but in its saying creates a place in which something can take place, something indistinguishable from what happens in the poem, the experience of a possibility.

One final thought about the poem and its feeling for human contingency: the etymology of the word "woe" and the structure of "Emergency Haying" have a similar development; "woe" began its career as a sound, a wail, and later acquired its spectrum of meanings—warning, denunciation, ruin, curse, grief, sorrow. The poem begins discursively as a private expression of pain and moves outward toward a public articulation of outrage in defense of the murdered, maimed and defiantly powerless. It goes from exhaustion to strength ("My strength is legion"), yet the strength isn't Christ's. Carruth draws his strength from those troubled spirits, the "legion" of "demoniacs" in Mark 5 who Christ cast out into swine. Carruth is drawn to these "unclean" and mad spirits, and he makes of that "legion," and all who belong to it, neighbors whose strength lies in their recognition of relatedness. Unlike Stevens the modernist who holds a solitary and Promethean vision of the artist, Carruth's transcending vision requires contingency and pure intercourse. Such a vision of ecstasy and communion occurs at the end of *Sitting In* — Carruth dreams of "a great session where race, or more properly speaking, ethnicity, has no significance at all, where 'culture' is irrelevant, where every performer or listener participates freely and equally in the bodily and spiritually wrenching, exhilarating, purging experience of jazz-in-itself." Take away jazz and substitute the medium of the poet, and one could say that this, too, was Whitman's American dream. "It cannot happen," writes Carruth, but one can hear Stevens's "and" in this skepticism. The dream is more powerful than its impossibility. The distinctive quality of Carruth's own voice resides in this wounded conjunction of vision and the impossibility of its realization. He might well have succumbed to its painfulness. And yet Carruth has heard its realization; as the final section of "Paragraphs" puts it:

                            for they had come
    high above themselves. Above everything, flux, ooze
    loss, need, shame, improbability/   the awfulness
    of gut-wrong,   sex-wrack,   horse & booze,
    the whole goddamn mess,
    And Gabler said "We'll press it"   and it was "Bottom Blues"
    BOTTOM BLUES   five men knowing it well   blacks & jews
    yet music, music   high
    in the celebration of fear, strange joy
    of pain: blown out, beaten out
                            a moment ecstatic

  in the history
  of creative mind and heart/   not singular, not the rarity
  we think, but real and a glory
  our human shining, shekinah …   Ah,
       holy spirit, ninefold
  I druther've bin a-settin there, supernumerary
  cockroach i'th'corner, a-listening, a-listening,,,,,,,,,
     than be the Prazedint ov the Wuurld.

"A-listening" he has heard it, and we know he has heard it, because, a-listening to him, we hear it too.

Anthony Robbins

Hyperborean Necessities: On *From Snow and Rock, From Chaos: Poems 1965–1972*

"North is ... nothing ..." (Carruth, "North Winter")
"There is too much of the north in me to be a man who complies entirely."
  (Andre Breton quoted by
  Carruth in "Who I Am")

Hayden Carruth is a peerless poet of the North, of the northern woods, of the western New England landscape that as a psychological paysage has been worked as thoroughly as the actual land. The husbandry of such a world is difficult, but neither Carruth's literary forebears—Emerson, Thoreau, Dickinson, Robinson, Millay, Frost, Scott—nor his neighbors—Francis, Lowell, Olson, Enslin, Booth, Kinnell, Ammons—have depleted the soil of nourishment for Carruth's particular crop. Though Carruth has explicitly and repeatedly abjured the ultra-Romantic notion of originality, his sense of his own extravagance and marginality, paired with his acute awareness of the necessities of responding to the social polity (both intimate and extensive) has resulted in poems that have a sparse, often severely dignified, pristine, a hyperboreal voice.

At the heart of Carruth's response to New England are the poems written during the middle of his first decade in Vermont and collected in *From Snow and Rock, From Chaos* (New Directions, 1973). These lyrics were written just after "Contra Mortem," and they are about erotic love, about family, about psychological incapacities and courages, and about the natural world. They give evidence of Carruth's assiduous training in a variety of lyric modes. In "Contra Mortem," a sequence of 30 "paragraphs," the 15-line sonnetto he invented and put to use in, among other poems, *The Sleeping Beauty* (1982), he used the vocabulary of European existentialism along with technical experiments such as omitting punctuation and running words together in an attempt, he has said, "to create a sequence that was philosophically acute and emotionally powerful." In *Snow* he continues to combine his "native Yankee pragmatism"

(Carruth on Thoreau) with his understanding of existentialism and of his place, Johnson, Lamoille County, Vermont. The poems collected here are some of his most cogent expressions of rebellion, necessity and "bestowal" (a word and a concept which he accepted from Irving Singer. See "Materials From Life," *Working Papers*). These are the coordinates of his nonviolent, existential anarchism.

Carruth is a Romantic thinker who has spent a lifetime exploring the destruction of the Romantic attraction to Beauty; he has wondered, "What/Is human 'authenticity' then but a nullity/ Striving to create value and getting beauty/Instead, dripping with blood. Will/Is the will to exploit" (*The Sleeping Beauty*). But it is beauty after all which Carruth achieves, though he despairs of the cost. In a poem written later than those in *Snow*, "Anima, for Janet," he talks about the unambiguous attractions of beauty:

> Firelight and starlight and woman,
> complete and beautiful, for only
> one place is known, ever, and this is
> there, meaning beauty, meaning
> all that is human in one fathoming,
> the passion of the mind, the reflectiveness
> of spirit. I do not know on this shore
> of a shadowed field in the shadow of my
> old age, what else a man lives for.

This hope, or rather, since Carruth has abjured the hope which abandons the present for the future, this expectancy, Keatsian in its equations, exists uncomfortably in a carnal nexus with Puritan denial and guilt. The pairing of eroticism and asceticism is central to Carruth's Yankee character. And the attempt to create that character brings him into the sugar shack with, among others, Robert Frost, the poet whom, Carruth has written, "is dominant in the American tradition, a figure with whom younger poets, even the most rebellious, must come to terms." He has also written, "I live where Frost lived./So? It's a free country. Don't/jump to conclusions." In *Snow*, Carruth responds to Frost. "Fear and Anger in the Mindless Universe" is strangely Frostian in voice; it has the best kind of Frostian perversity and ambiguity. A Vermonter, Evan, is walking to cambridge junction (uncapitalized like many of the proper nouns in this book) when he witnesses a car crashing and then watches furtively as "the stranger" bleeds to death

>   in ten minutes
> though the ice patch weren't his fault
>   and Evan began to feel better—
> he even begun to laugh.
>   That was last tuesday week in the forenoon
> but now
>   he tells it without smiling
> quicklike
>   looking out of the corner of his eye.

Despite the unusual rhythm created by the broken lines, the diction is Frostian, New England in terseness as well as in vernacular. As an exemplum of fear and anger in the mindless universe, the action, or the inaction, is disturbingly effective. Evan lives in the same redneck fear and anger as the Miller in Frost's "The Vanishing Red," which is, on Carruth's account, one of Frost's best. The connection between Evan and the Miller is their inhumanity, their nihilism. The Miller put the Indian down into the wheel housing, and

> Then he shut down the trap door with a ring in it
> That jangled even above the general noise,
> And came upstairs alone—and gave that laugh.

Carruth thinks this is the climax of the poem, "the Miller's laugh, and what that laugh means is the heart of Frost's poetic temperament: the blackest, bitterest despair in three hundred years of the New England Tradition." He suggests that the despair is radically Puritan, the vision of man in self-made hell. "It is the greatest absurdity, as our survival, somehow in spite of it, our blind, ceaseless endurance, is the greatest heroism." If there is a Faulknerian quality to this feeling, that is because the Miller's and Evan's laughter are much like Jason Compson's. Evan's laugh is less malevolent and more reprehensible than the Miller's. Fear of death makes him angry. Anger paralyzes his will to act. He loses all intention. He becomes nothing. And why is he afraid of seeing death, a death? Because he is a Puritan. In an essay on Robert Lowell, the best on its subject, Carruth explains the genesis of this, the

> ultimate Yankee metonymy ... Puritan death as punishment for sin contracts, under the paradox of benign transcendentalism, to death as sin. Naturally it is a theological monstrosity. It is impossible. Yet in the human and poetic sphere, it is a validity of staggering force. And it lies at the heart of the American sensibility ....
>
> ("A Meaning of Robert Lowell," *Working Papers*)

This comes from Carruth's reading of Lowell's "Night Sweat," and this feeling about death as guilt emerges in two lines in the middle of it: "always inside me is the child who died,/always inside me is his will to die." This "impossible necessary death" (Maurice Blanchot's term) is absurd, but in order for speech, for action, to occur, the infant must have been killed—by the speaker. Thus we advance by suicide/murder, without assuming direct responsibility for it, *but* not without guilt. In Evan's case, his murderous inaction makes him "feel better" at once, but because his fear of that death was real, guilt grows in him, driving him even further than he is from communion. He looks "out of the corner of his eye," the way shades in the *Inferno* look at one another: invidiously, without trust, with envy. They look at one another askance: with ask-ance, asking for forgiveness and identity, but getting neither. In his spiritual isolation Evan is the genius of the notches and gulfs of the Green Mountains.

Carruth's conversations with Frost are clearly evident in other poems of this period. "The Existing Pool" (*Dark World*, 1973) can be seen as Carruth's (re)version of Frost's "For Once, Then, Something." Both have the same conventional topic: a man looks into the water and sees, mainly, himself. Frost's poem moves very deliberately from the general habitual activity of looking to a somewhat more specific experience, which reveals a glimpse of "Truth? A pebble of quartz? For once, then, something." Carruth has written that he feels the poem was "faked," that the "Truth" of the final line destroys any veracity in the poem's ostensible search ("Robert Frost," *Effluences*). Carruth's poem begins at a real pool, "below the Shinglemill Bridge." The symbolic valence of the elements — pebbles on the bottom, the clarity of the water, reflections of face and sky — are resisted by Carruth as much as they are asserted in Frost's poem. This resistance is a reflection of Carruth's vision of human intelligence: separate, across the fence, as it were, from the rest of nature. In contrast to the speaker's vision in Frost's poem —"something," "whatever it was," "blurred"— Carruth sees with great acuity the particular elements of nature, but the images themselves have

> neither originality
> nor grace, and the others too,
> these inventions of yours,
> guardian trees, mosaics, windows, dancing—
> all absent. Reality and unreality
> are your ways of looking into the pool
> for the pool has neither.
> The pool "has" nothing at all.

And of course neither does the "you" *except* as love, work, and lucidity create a unity in which the fragments of personality cohere.

> Liebe, our light rekindles
> in this remoteness from the other land,
> in this dark of the winter mountain where only
> the winds gather
>
> is what we are for the time that we are
> what we know for the time that we know
>
> How gravely and sweetly the poor touch in the dark.
>
> ("If It Were Not For You," *Snow*)

This kind of coherence through erotic solidarity has to be established not only in a place but in a time. In "Contra Mortem" Carruth made meaning from the elements of human apperception of time. Here, in "The Ravine" for example, time is apprehended as the measure of change. The poem begins as a description of the still life of the ravine: weeds, mink, snake, dead woodcock — the moment. Then the poet remembers:

>   in spring it
> cascaded, in winter it filled with snow
> until it lay hidden completely. In time,
> geologic time, it will melt away
> or deepen beyond recognition, a huge
> gorge. These are what I remember and foresee.
> These are what I see here everyday,
> not things but relationships of things,
> quick changes and slow. These are my sorrow,
> for unlike my bright admonitory friends
> I see relationships, I do not see things.
> These, such as they are, every day, every
> unique day, the first in time and the last,
> are my thoughts, the sequences of my mind.
> I wonder what they mean. Every day,
> day after day, I wonder what they mean.

Moment, memory, prevision are bestowed upon reality. They reveal the ravine as they create the pace and the meaning of the poem. The tone, characteristic of Carruth, is querulous and elegiac. To see things in relationship is to see them changed. To wonder why and to feel their loss. The thing-in-itself does not exist. The objective moment is, in art and in the artless encountering of the world, illusion. In terms of representation this means that the relationships in the verbal world of the poem (though of course not a world unrelated to other worlds) *are* the sequences of the poet's mind, not symbolic of them.

In his review of *Brothers I Loved You All* (*American Poetry Review*), Philip Booth articulates the source of Carruth's insistence upon relationships, his radical relativism.

> But nothing is entirely "in itself" when met by the poet. In the poet's consciousness of his *relationship* to the actual, what's ordinary becomes extraordinary as it is raised by the power of a voice (however quiet) which verifies the music of time's inconstant constancy. Because poetry assumes time (as painting

and sculpture assume space), poetry is by nature elegiac: by timing itself (through every tactic of rhythm, caesura, resonance, recurrence, pace, etc.) to make present the immediacy of a time out of time, a poem celebrates both its own temporal nature and (paradoxically) the timeless vitality of its own being.

This is a clairvoyant appraisal of what Carruth has done in "The Ravine" and in many other poems in *Snow*. Carruth's existential concept of lucidity—that is, keeping obliteration, the end of a time, ever in mind—coincides with the way that a poem must necessarily unfold in time. It is the same way that a personality accretes, toward extinction. Poetry assumes time and so it assumes the end of a time. Death is in fact the mother of this beauty.

Carruth's pairing of lucidity and romance is unique in American poetry; it reveals the tension between the opposing claims of experience and imagination (and here he encounters Stevens and others). A resolution of this tension occurs as the poet combines freedom and discipline in making the poem. Carruth respects the integrity both of things and of words, and this creates a special dilemma when the imagination tries to see itself in the natural world, that old Romantic bugaboo. Carruth tries to admit the thing and the emotional valence of the thing and thereby to show the dynamics of the collision. In "I Know, I Remember, But How Can I Help You" a doe's presence under the northern lights becomes a moment which, greeted by the wonderful yearning of the man, is complicated by all of the elements of being: memory, moment, prevision; by beauty, fear, desire, remorse. And inevitable solitude:

> I remember   but without the sense   other light-
>   storms
> cold memories discursive and philosophical
>   in my mind's burden
> and the deer remembers nothing.
> We move on our feet   crunching bitter snow   while the storm
> crashes like god-wars down the east
>   we shake the sparks from our eyes
> we quiver inside our shocked fur
>   we search for each other

>   in the apple thicket—
>   a glimpse, an acknowledgement
>   it is enough and never enough—
>   we toss our heads   and say goodnight
>   moving away on bitter bitter snow.

The supernumerary nature of human intelligence, even as it is conscious of its distance from others, does not preclude its need to find correspondence with the doe's atemporal imagination. A world is imperfectly shared; it is "enough and never enough." Impossible for either to come all the way into the spirit of the other. The pragmatic character of Carruth's mind compels him in the transaction between imagination and reality to realize the limits of both, limits which potentiate the entire exchange. The personalizing urge insists that he negotiate the schism, but historical knowledge and self-consciousness only let him do so up to a point. To collapse the distinctions is morally and therefore aesthetically untenable. Poetry is an act of creative imagination which is an act of personality, an act of love which embraces the inner and the outer void. It is like the strange thing given to the speaker of "This Decoration":

>   How
>   exquisite, flowers
>
>   of imagination from this
>   real world, made and given
>   for lovingkindness

The poem exists both as a time and as a place where change and mutual affirmation can justifiably occur. This notion is as central as any to Carruth's poetics;

> It [poetry] returns from the frontiers of experience bearing chaos and revolution, the rawness of events, which it submits to the regulative conceptualizing of our permanent, concrete, basic, human modes; that is, to language.
>
> It follows that poetry is social, though not in any sense of the term used by sociologists. It follows then that poetry is political, leaving the political scientists far behind. Maybe it even follows

> that if the substance of a poem, or part of it is expressly though broadly social or political, this fact will reinforce the subjective communalism of the poet's intention in his transcendental act; but that is a question – the interrelationship of substance and the vision of form, or of moral and aesthetic feeling – to which twenty-five years of attention have given me no answer ... Finally it follows that the politics of the poet, in his spirituality, will be a politics of love. For me this means non-violent anarchism, at least as a means; I know no end. For others it means something else. But we will share, at least in our spirituality, far more than we will dispute.
> (*Working Papers*)

Carruth rejects deliberate assumptions of (and sadly abhors de facto) artistic autonomy. He insists on the demands of experience,

> that only a poet who remains open to experience – and not only open, but submissive, and not only to experience, but to the actual newness of experience here and now – only such a poet can hope to repeat his successes.
> (*Effluences From the Sacred Caves*)

Also in evidence of his dependence on an experiential core are his comments on R.P. Blackmur's dictum that poetic language should "add to the stock of available reality," an idea which was taken up enthusiastically (and in Carruth's account disastrously) by poets, most prominently by John Berryman. Language, Carruth says, cannot create meaning. This is a fallacy which he has tried to resist in his poetry. It is a temptation to which Carruth without doubt, given his huge verbal facilities, has been often inclined. His resistance to merely verbal realities is deliberate: entre-les-guerres modernism revised in light of post-war existentialism. Reviewing *Snow*, Wendell Berry wrote,

> When the worlds of so many poets are made out of words, as though poetry were accessible to no more than talent and ambition, it is a moving affirmation of the power of poetry that *Snow* does not make a world of its own. It does not attempt or desire to do so. Instead it accepts the obligations of the world outside itself that it did not make.
> (*American Poetry Review*)

Berry puts the emphasis on necessities and obligations. As Booth remarks, Carruth's imagination, like Stevens', struggles with reality, with "the necessary angel." But, more than Stevens, Carruth admits fortuity. "Fortuity" is as loaded a word as "necessity" in Carruth's technical vocabulary. His elaboration of the concept originates in *After The Stranger: Imaginary Dialogues with Camus* (1965). Camus, the character, asserts in response to Aspen's need for an external source of strength (Dora) that love leading to true solidarity is fortuitous, rare, because sex is grounded in physiological not ethical necessity. Erotic solidarity is a fortuitous, not a necessary consequence of "love."

The tensions between fortuity and necessity are apparent in "Abandoned Ranch, Big Bend." The boreal sensibilities of the speaker, restless even when incorporate in their native New England, are here in the desert raw-ripe as an ovary. The normal limitations of the senses have been burned away, as if they were skin, and the self seems to be dissolved in a kind of helpless solution with the acrid, ominous landscape:

> Summoned
> From half across the world, from snow and rock,
> From chaos, they arrived a moment ago, they thought,
> In perfect fortuity ...

The poem concludes:

> Again and again among the dry
> Wailing voices of misplaced Yankee ghosts
> This ranch is abandoned to terror and the sublime.
> The man turns to the woman and the child. He has never
> Said what he meant. They give him
> The steady cool mercy of their unreproachful eyes.

Here in the stark light of the desert the speaker feels (historically) the impossibility of perfect expression of self in language, which has material and formal limits unknown to the spirit. He cannot say what he means. The mercies of his family cannot help. There is inevitable distance. Distance means solitude, but the persistence of distance, no matter how close the other seems, also creates a poignance, an eternal aura which always attracts, always presents the fortuitous possibility of wholeness. Carruth's gift at bodying forth this aura is strongly evident in the poem that is at the spiritual core of this essential book: "Concerning Necessity."

It is a tenet of existentialism (if such a thing can be said to exist) that the existence of the other makes the self possible. Kierkegaard, so seminal for many existential concepts, clearly said this:

> For the purpose of becoming (and it is the task of the self freely to become itself) possibility and necessity are equally essential.

Possibility is, by definition, abstract and infinite (and monolithic). Necessities are material and for anyone who must work for a living seemingly infinite in kind and in number. But Carruth knows that necessity, especially necessity driven by erotic desire—that is, work done not for the corporate state, or, abstractly, for the community at large, but work done for those whom we love—that kind of necessity can create a world where we can live, committed *and* free. His vision of this world is nowhere more apparent than in "Concerning Necessity," where the tiring daily life of a man in the hills of Vermont is made to reveal an aura of almost unbearable beauty.

> It's quite true we live
> in a kind of rural twilight
> most of the time giving
> our love to the hard dirt
> the water and the weeds
> and the difficult woods
>
> ho we say drive the wedge
> heave the axe run the hand shovel
> dig the potato patch
> dig ashes dig gravel
> tickle the dyspeptic chainsaw
> make him snarl once more

while the henhouse needs cleaning
the fruitless corn to be cut
and the house is falling to pieces
the car coming apart
the boy sitting and complaining
about something everything anything

this was the world foreknown
though I had thought somehow
probably in the delusion
of that idiot thoreau
that necessity could be saved
by the facts we actually have

like our extreme white birch
clasped in the hemlock's arms
or our bay-breasted nuthatch
or our mountains and our stars
and really these things do serve
a little though not enough

what saves the undoubted collapse
of the driven day and the year
is my coming all at once
when she is done in or footsore
or down asleep in the field
or telling a song to a child

coming and seeing her move
in some particular way
that makes me to fall in love
all over with human beauty
the beauty I can't believe
right here where I live

    The speaker spends most of his time giving his time and his energy and therefore his love to his small holding of land in order to make his life out of "the hard dirt/the water and the weeds/and the difficult woods." By means of the "and's" in stanza one, Carruth has mimetically created the fatigue of the speaker. As Longinus, the writer whom Carruth admires "maybe most of all" notes, polysyndeton is effective because emotion frets at being impeded by conjunctions and other additions, because it loses free abandon of its movement and the sense of being, as it were, catapulted out.

The loss of abandon creates a discipline, creates the possibility of beauty. The emotions are not catapulted out into the realm of possibility, but harmonized in the straits of necessity. The opposite figure, asyndeton, omission of conjunctions, connotes the urgency of chores in the third stanza. Yet these chores are the real occasion for this song, "ho we say drive the wedge/heave the axe ..." Intimacy with one's tools causes even the loud, stinking, tree-eating saw to become familiar, almost an extension of the viscera. The fact of hard labor was foreknown. This is and has always been the fact of life in the woods, but the speaker had shared with Thoreau the delusion that nature alone could be a tonic, could actually mitigate necessity. To say that "necessity could be saved/by the facts we actually have" means at least two ways: natural facts—trees, birds, mountains, stars, and the fact of our contemplation of them—can mitigate the pain of necessity; it also means that these facts are where necessity is saved; we find our necessity in them and also therefore the potential of self-creation. The trees are, as ever in Carruth's poetry, a large part of this complementary natural cohort. The hemlocks are lovers; they have arms. This is a vision of trees that persists from Carruth's early poems in *The Bloomingdale Papers*. The anthropomorphism comes from living with the trees, and personification calls into question how it is that we can *have* facts, *our* mountain, *our* stars. Can human intelligence *have* anything except on its own terms, in terms of itself? Perhaps this is impossible, but we should resist the tendency to wholly expropriate; we should be practical and metaphysical stewards of the world. Nature is not to be overcome, but is, instead, a sometimes difficult, sometimes compliant partner. Nature is necessary, but not sufficient, not enough. In the sixth stanza necessity is apposite to "the undoubted collapse/of the driven day and the year," that is, the realm of necessity encompasses both work and time, and the end of time, death. Time constrains and defines life by giving it a term. Man must rebel against the collapse of time (collapse short of death caused by anger, arrogance, guilt) by imposing his own order. This is where existentialism and romanticism concur: Camus, in a Blakean mode, has written, "Genius is a rebellion that has created its own limits." But these limits are not created solely by or for the self. Here the "she" of the poem becomes a necessity because of her own demonstrations of love. The speaker is *made* "to fall in love/all over with human beauty," meaning to fall once again, but also that he is encompassed in his own compassionate reaction and is therefore beautiful. The rather awkward syntax here ("makes me to fall in love") indicates at once the "choked up" moment of epiphany. It also indicates with "makes" 1) that there is a certain passivity on the part of the speaker, 2) that this moment is when personality is made, or 3) created for the purpose of that moment, i.e., "Makes me for the purpose of falling in love," and, 4) the deliberate and unusual adjacency of the pronoun "me" to the infinitive "to fall" indicates that this moment is the interstice of the finite person with the infinite possibility of action. The climax of the poem creates a confluence of the actual (me) with the possible (to fall), issuing forth in the necessity which is the claim of the title. This necessity is the incredible beauty: his chaotic being and hers, endowed with a unity. It is immediate and contingent, only here in the spot of time in which he stands. Insofar as the speaker can respond to beauty, he is, and must be, dedicated to this time, this place, to the present, to "what we are for the time that we are/what we know for the time that we know."

 This beauty is in service of one of Carruth's characteristic themes, the relationship of art and the artist to the world at large. Camus, who is important to Carruth in many ways, has put it forcibly: "Art rejects the world on account of what it lacks and in the name of what it sometimes is." The world often lacks love, so the questing of man must be for love. Life is essentially erotic, an erotic struggle that finds its ultimate form in art, "in a poetry that, by the very tension of its striving, confutes the recurrent social philosophies of expedience and claptrap." The existentialist lives in the name of this struggle and of the occasional beauty in man that is discovered through lucid attention to the present and through work. Camus makes a connection between this existential aesthetic and the aesthetics of transcendentalism:

> There is a living transcendence, of which beauty carries the promise, which can make this mortal and limited world preferable to and more appealing than any other.

From Snow and Rock, From Chaos is full of this living transcendence, full of the beauty and the promises that a lucid mind in service of peace and restraint can fulfill.

Stephen Kuusisto

Elegiac Locales: The Anarchy of Hayden Carruth

I.

Poets have always read nature as a text for transcendence, but following World War II, the natural world was no longer a "de profundis" muse. The poet's relationship to landscape had changed: henceforth it would have to be defined and enacted in the context of post-atomic industry. Poets as diverse as Kenneth Rexroth, Yvor Winters, and Gary Snyder created locales in which a careful enumeration of geographies and human actions furnished a primer or blueprint for merely living—an aesthetic *realpolitik* which has roots in nineteenth century anarchist principles.

Many anarchists were surveyors and map makers. Kropotkin was a geographer. His encounters with rural people who faced adversity through cooperative efforts furnished proof that nature might still be our school. Reading *Mutual Aid*, one sees that work and community are the means by which human beings *create* human nature: the farmer, the builder, even the doctor—all confirm through their work that value derives from serving the land and the community. Every human action thereby reflects the dignity of work. No idea was more crucial to the American communalist tradition which tried to build a new Eden. Anarchy depended on the belief that human beings are part of an organic community and that the proper aim of culture is to live in a creative, non-exploitative relationship with our neighbors and the environment. The key to this lay in our working lives.

The aesthetic and political impact of these concerns have influenced recent American poetry in diverse ways. Robert Bly settled on a farm in Minnesota and wrote *Silence in the Snowy Fields*, a book which celebrates rural solitude. In Gary Snyder's *Earth House Hold*, working in the mountains or in the merchant marine is only partly an aesthetic experience: labor is often a paradigm for human franchise. Workers become citizens, freethinkers, and "Dharma Bums." Their exertions in the service of ecology are also exercises in meditation. In this way "culture" is restored to its earliest meaning. Snyder's essay "The Yogin and the Philosopher" argues that caring for the environment has been the nucleus of our ancestors' labors. Robert Bly, Galway Kinnell, Thomas McGrath, Hayden Carruth, and Wendell Berry have all written poems and essays which link farming and conservation with the craft of writing.

II.

Hayden Carruth's rural narratives make connections between landscape and individual character. Farming is hard, talking is hard, the erosions of traditional ways of life are insurmountable. The farms Carruth knows and works are small, marginal, almost worn out. The acreage won't sustain much capital investment in machinery or labor. By enumerating the passing of small Yankee farms, Carruth's poems record the disappearance of essential knowledge and, in a sense, become elegies to the kind of life that Kropotkin once envisioned in *Mutual Aid*. The passing of a cooperative, rural, social and economic order is contiguous with the despoiling of the environment: the people who know the land and tend it have been bought out or foreclosed. *Brothers, I Loved You All* contains a series of meditations on these themes.

In "Marshall Washer" Carruth presents the works and days of a struggling, solitary northern Vermont farmer who is also the poet's neighbor and friend. The work "breaks the farmers' backs./It makes their land./It is the link eternal, binding man and beast/and earth." This is Carruth's appreciation for a man who knows the land and tends it, and the poem provides a glimpse of labor as a locus or point of connection between mind, life, and nature. Farming is the act of *making*:

> I see a man in bib overalls
> and rubber boots kneeling in cowshit to smear
> ointment on a sore teat, a man with a hayfork,
> a dungfork, an axe, a 20-pound maul
> for driving posts, a canthook, a grease gun.

> I see a man notching a cedar post
> with a double-bladed axe, rolling the post
> under his foot in the grass: quick strokes and there
> is a ringed groove one inch across, as clean
> as if cut with the router blade down at the mill.

In "Marshall Washer" craftsmanship is synonymous with assiduousness and spirit. Marshall's handicraft reflects his engagement with trials and tests. In a sense, Marshall's work may be understood as an essay and the poem's theme is in the relationship between farmer and poet. Carruth has been Marshall's neighbor and friend, as well as his student. By becoming his historian he articulates the unwritten essay of Marshall's life. In turn, the poem becomes an essay on work, cooperation, landscape, and poetry:

>   I have written
> of Marshall often, for his presence is in my poems
> as in my life, so familiar that it is not named;
> yet I have named him sometimes too, in writing
> as in life, gratefully. We are friends. Our friendship
> began when I came here years ago, seeking
> what I had once known in southern New England,
> now destroyed. I found it in Marshall, among others.
> He is friend and neighbor both, an important
> distinction. His farm is one-hundred-eighty acres
> (plus a separate woodlot of forty more), and one
> of the best-looking farms I know, sloping smooth
> pastures, elm-shaded knolls, a brook, a pond,
> his woods of spruce and pine, with maples and oaks
> along the road—not a showplace, not by any means,
> but a working farm with fences of old barbed wire;
> no pickets, no post-and-rail. His cows are Jerseys.
> My place, no farm at all, is a country laborer's
> holding, fourteen acres "more or less" (as the deed
> says), but we adjoin. We have no fence. Marshall's
> cows graze in my pasture; I cut my fuel
> in his woods. That's neighborliness. And when
> I came here Marshall taught me ... I don't know,
> it seems like everything: how to run a barn,
> make hay, build a wall, make maple syrup
> without a trace of bitterness, a thousand things.

> (Though I thought I wasn't ignorant when I came,
> and I wasn't—just three-quarters informed.
> You know how good a calf is, born three-legged.)
> In fact half my life now, I mean literally half,
> is spent in actions I could not perform without
> his teaching. Yet it wasn't teaching; he *showed* me.
> Which is what makes all the difference. In return
> I gave a hand, helped in the fields, started
> frozen engines, mended fence, searched for lost calves,
> picked apples for the cider mill, and so on.
> And Marshall, alone now, often shared my table.
> This too is neighborliness.

The poem assays neighborliness, sorrow, age and loss—the intangibles from which lives are achieved. The knowledge Carruth acquires from Marshall is functional, but his awareness that there are distinctions to be made between "neighbor" and "friend" alerts the reader that the poem is engaged in an intricate "weighing" of values. To "name" Marshall is to conjure his presence as a figure who works side by side with the poet: together they tend the land and share what's in common. Writing about Marshall becomes an exercise in discrimination: the precise values of words and actions must be arrived at. Carruth aims for exactitude—literal meanings—and the poem seeks to establish whatever distinctions can be made between terms like "neighbor" and "friend" because in naming Marshall, Carruth is hoping to preserve the propriety and right-mindedness of a man whose world is on the verge of extinction.

Accordingly, we learn that friendship can be built from silence, or it can persist when conversation is provisional. For Carruth, whose "art" is contingent upon the spoken and written word, Marshall's silence provides a lesson in "reading" a man. It's a curious, ascetic's world that Carruth explores, and the poem's language works toward similitude in its precise accounting of both Marshall's vernacular and his silence. The accuracy of Marshall's language and Carruth's curiosity about its etymology makes this a memorable tribute to a friend:

> I see a man who studied by lamplight, the journals
> and bulletins, new methods, struggling to buy
> equipment, forty years to make his farm
> a good one; alone now, his farm the last
> on Clay Hill, where I myself remember ten.
> He says "I didn't mind it" for "I didn't notice it,"
> "dreened" for "drained," "climb" (pronounced *climm*)
> for "climbed," "stanchel" for "stanchion,"
> and many other unfamiliar locutions; but I
> have looked them up, they are in the dictionary,
> standard speech of lost times. He is rooted
> in history as in the land, the only man I know
> who lives in the house where he was born. I see
> a man alone walking his fields and woods,
> knowing every useful thing about them, moving
> in a texture of memory that sustains his lifetime
> and his father's lifetime. I see a man
> falling asleep at night with thoughts and dreams
> I could not infer – and would not if I could –
> in his chair in front of his television.

Marshall's language is accurate: his "texture of memory" makes him a guide – a person who informs the poet by example. Carruth trusts Marshall's silence and, as a consequence, learns to make distinctions between "talk" and "articulation". The latter is a junction: a marriage, a concurrence, and people who use words sparingly may possess it. The former is profuse and digressive, something the poet learns to distrust:

> Marshall and I
> worked ten years together, and more than once
> in hardship. I remember the late January
> when his main gave out and we carried water,
> hundreds and thousands of gallons, to the heifers
> in the upper barn (the one that burned next summer),
> then worked inside the well to clear the line
> in temperatures that rose to ten below
> at noonday. We knew such times. Yet never
> did Marshall say the thought that was closest to him.
> Privacy is what this is; not reticence, not
> minding one's own business, but a positive sense

>   of the secret inner man, the sacred identity.
>   A man is his totem, the animal of his mind.
>   Yet I was angered sometimes. How could friendship
>   share a base so small of mutual substance?
>   Unconsciously I had taken friendship's measure
>   from artists everywhere who had been close to me,
>   people living for the minutest public dissection
>   of emotion and belief. But more warmth was
>   and is, in Marshall's quiet "hello" than in all
>   those others and their wordiest protestations,
>   more warmth and far less vanity.

I'm reminded here of Santayana's notion of "animal faith"–human instinct, that "animal" of the mind, is a kind of forbearance against the quotidian. By rejecting silence as dismissal or unconcern, Carruth also rejects language which is overtly designing, the glib chatter of our age, and insists that knowing another human being depends on reception, harmony, and cooperation. Making the distinction between privacy and reticence allows Carruth to more accurately estimate the nature of friendship. It's no coincidence that in defining this he also underscores ecological values: the sacred identity, the man as totem is properly "in" the world.

In a very real sense, the poem is much more than a tribute to a teacher. Carruth's precise estimation of Marshall allows for a reciprocal interaction between the subject of the poem and the making of a poem. Marshall is both the inspiring muse of the poem as well as the figure being "assayed". This becomes an essay on human cooperation, the value of friendship, and the importance of deliberation and judgement in our dealings with our fellows and the environment.

III.

The "elegiac" character of *Brothers, I Loved You All* is in the poems' careful listings of the many extinctions that have happened in our time. Carruth writes: "This/has been the time of the finishing off of the animals./They are going away–their fur and their wild eyes,/their voices." Elsewhere he says with a laconic twist: "The weak/have conquered and the valley is their domain." The farms and the topography of Vermont have been sold to "predatory" developers. Carruth describes "bulldozers, at least of the imagination":

>   The hilltop farms are going.
> Bottomland farms, mechanized, are all that survive.
> As more and more developers take over
> northern Vermont, values of land increase,
> taxes increase, farming is an obsolete vocation—
> while half the world goes hungry. Marshall walks
> his fields and woods, knowing every useful thing
> about them, and knowing his knowledge useless.
> Bulldozers, at least of the imagination,
> are poised to level every knoll, to strip bare
> every pasture. Or maybe a rich man will buy it
> for a summer place. Either way the link
> of the manure, that had seemed eternal, is broken.
> Marshall is not young now. And though I am only
> six or seven years his junior, I wish somehow
> I could buy the place, merely to assure him
> that for these few added years it might continue—
> drought, flood, or depression. But I am too
> ignorant, in spite of his teaching. This is more
> than a technocratic question. I cannot smile
> his quick sly Yankee smile in sorrow,
> nor harden my eyes with the true granitic resistance
> that shaped this land. How can I learn the things
> that are not transmissible? Marshall knows them.
> He possesses them, the remnant of human worth
> to admire in this world, and I think to envy.

In the end, all knowledge is particular, its acquisition comes in bits and pieces, and it can't be hurried. Marshall's "granitic resistance" and taciturnity represent both concealment and revelation: the signs of a life shaped by work and weather. Carruth explores the complex relationship between the making of a farm and the "texture of memory that sustains [Marshall's] lifetime/and his father's lifetime." The poet reads that texture and deciphers it. The effect of Carruth's writing is perhaps reflected in Carlyle's assertion that "In Symbol there is concealment and yet revelation: here therefore, by Silence and by Speech acting together, comes a double significance." These poems lament the passing of something more intangible than the farms. The "remnant of human worth" is recorded in the poem's description of lost trades and vanished skills:

>   He sows
> his millet broadcast, swinging left to right,
> a half-acre for the cows' "fall tonic" before
> they go in the barn for good: an easy motion,
> slow swinging, a slow dance in the field, and just
> the opposite, right to left, for the scythe
> or the brush hook. Yes, I have seen such dancing
> by a man alone in the slant of the afternoon.
> At his anvil with his big smith's hammer
> he can pound shape back in a wagon iron, or tap
> a butternut so it just lies open.

When Carruth enumerates the ways of knowing that have vanished he's as precise as Hardy, as direct as any Yankee. We see the farms broken up and their owners driven off even as we're hearing the local speech. In this locale there is a life-supporting relationship between language, landscape, and character.

Sam Hamill

Listening In

"The great contribution of the twentieth century to art is the idea of spontaneous improvisation within a determined style, a style comprising equally or inseparably both conventional and personal elements. What does this mean? It means a great deal more than the breakup of traditional prosody or rules of composition, as announced in 1910 by Ezra Pound and Pablo Picasso. It means the final abandonment of the neo-classical idea of structure as a function of form, which the romantics and post-romantics of the nineteenth century had never given up. Instead structure has become a function of feeling." So saith Hayden Carruth in a marvelous essay on Pee Wee Russell and Willie Yeats collected with other poems and essays in *Sitting In: Selected Writings on Jazz, Blues, and Related Topics* (University of Iowa Press, 1986).

"Form," Robert Creeley observes, "is never more than an extension of content." Which Denise Levertov clarifies, "Form is the revelation of content." Carruth's idea of structure as a function of feeling enlarges and clarifies something that has been at the center of critical philosophy most of this century.

Picasso's cubism grew out of his study of African art as surely as the Blues grew out of African music transplanted in the New World. And the idea of spontaneous improvisation within a determined style is at least as old as the *Shih Ching*, the *Classic of Poetry* Confucius compiled 2500 years ago. Perhaps the greatest literary contribution of the Sung dynasty a thousand years ago is the elevation of *tzu*, a verse-form wherein the poet composes new lyrics for a pre-existing tune. The form reached its pinnacle in the poetry of Li Ch'ing-chao. But the *structure* of the poem was an externally fixed form based upon musical measure. Carruth is seeking a structure from within.

"Genius," William Blake said, opening English poetry to a whole universe found in a grain of sand, "is not lawless."

Ezra Pound insisted that the line in poetry be composed "by the musical phrase and not by the metronome." Hayden Carruth, that perennial jazz *aficionado* and compulsive "woodshedder," understands Pound's dictum probably as well as anyone presently writing poetry in the U.S. of A. "Improvisation," Carruth says elsewhere in the same book, "is the privilege of the master, the bane of the apprentice. It is the exercise of sensibility in acquired knowledge. When it becomes too often repeated, either in the work of the master or later in that of his followers, it loses spontaneity, because nothing of freshness is happening and then it is over. Done .... Improvisation then is composition, but composition impelled by knowledgeable spirit ...."

And what is the spirit of the master? And how does the poem arise from one's deepest and most sincere practice? A composition impelled by knowledgeable spirit? It might take the form of poetry by Robert Duncan, or by Denise Levertov, the former still read only by a handful of poets, the latter rather grudgingly granted status as a major poet by a fickle, ignorant public. That we prefer the simple and immediately recognizable in all things can be seen perfectly clearly in the rise of the national fast food chain, in best seller lists, in the idiocy of American television and its movie-star politicians, and in our poetry anthologies.

The "knowledgeable spirit" arises out of long-standing practice of "woodshedding" what Duncan called "the scales of the marvelous" or by seeking what Carruth has called "wisdom that is the ghost of wisdom, otherwise called humility before one's task." So that the real task of the poet is to bring the whole of one's life into the presence of disciplined improvisation within a measure, whether that measure be fixed from within or without, or whether that measure is variable, as in the case of William Carlos Williams's "variable foot" which brought Charles Olson to observe that "a foot is for kicking."

"To break the back of the iamb, that was the first heave."
(Ezra Pound)

Well. It sagged, it bent, but it didn't break. And it won't break as long as we choose to place greater stress upon one syllable than upon another with any degree of regularity: the iamb is the foundation of our spoken music. And it is precisely the flexibility of our tongue that makes it one of the finest poetic languages in the world, capable of compression and expansion, capable of working within externally fixed measures like the metronome (based upon the heartbeat?) and more "organic" measures such as the breath or ear alert to vowel-weights and the durations of syllables rather than their stresses. As poets, we are invited to learn the Greek resonating vowel-scale, the syllabus of elementary linguistics, the regulated syllabic lines which were the foundation upon which our literary ancestors constructed our English heritage, the open motion of "rowing poetry" (as Robert Graves identified it) as opposed to "hammer-and-anvil measures" (which were the source, according to Graves, of that same iambic ancestry). In brief, our melopoeia is among the most sophisticated and most resonant in the world. But, like our most important gift to the arts of the world, North American jazz, its supreme beauty is far more widely understood elsewhere in the world than by the general public (even the literary public) at home.

Graves's research into prosody divides poetry into these two basic measures. But we might also divide poetry into two other categories: 1) the lyric or *sincere* mode; and 2) the bardic or narrative mode. In the latter (as for instance in Chaucer), the tale may or may not be formed primarily by the exercise of exterior structure; but in the former, a flexibility is mandatory since feeling or emotion is paramount because the poet is searching out the *structure of feeling*. The flexibility of the classical Greek line accommodated, inspired, a grandly lyrical form. Or as Carruth, a sincere poet, says, "Structure is a *function* of feeling."

In 1982, Hayden Carruth published a masterpiece, *The Sleeping Beauty*, a minor epic of one-hundred-twenty-four choruses built upon a fifteen-line movement grounded in pentameter and interior and end rhyme and slant rhyme. It is a form he first began exploring in a suite of thirteen poems, "The Asylum," in his first book, *The Crow and the Heart* (Macmillan, 1959), but a quarter-century of woodshedding has transformed this variation on the sonnet into a measure entirely his own. More flexible because of its irregular syllabics, the form isn't as emotionally or melodically confined as the sonnet.

The poem itself is a long meditation on the exploitation of woman and the natural world through stubbornly naive romanticism, including the poet's own, since the poem is itself a kind of romance. The "sleeping beauty" of the poem is Rose Marie Dorn, the poet's wife, whose dreams insistently involve men with names beginning with the letter *H*,– Homer, Hesiod, Hannibal, Hegel, Hitler, and, not incidentally, the historical/philosophical horrors of Hermaphroditism, the Holocaust, and the Hydrogen bomb. Interwoven among her dreams, there is a narrative structure, as much philosophical as literal, and often articulated in anecdotal passages narrated by a northeastern back-country prophet named Amos. The devices are many and sophisticated.

Opening the poem, beginning "out of nothing" (and with a "nothing" carried over from an epigraph from Goethe's "Vanitas! Vanitatum Vanitas!"), Carruth sets his scene and invokes his muse:

> ...
> The word is silent ...
>   Oh, begin
> In all and nothing then, the vision from a name,
> This Rose Marie Dorn,
> Woman alive exactly when the Red Army came
> To that crook of the Oder where she was born,
> Woman who fled and fled in her human duty
> And bore her name, meaning Rose in the Thorn,
> Her name, the mythologos, the Sleeping Beauty. (#3)

But this is no neo-Byronic declaration of eternally adolescent love-worship. Carruth's most obvious ancestor is Pound, and it is in the mode of the *Cantos* that Carruth seeks to join his narrative with his lyric. "Let the song," he says in his fifth chorus, "Sing, from that inward stress, this world so surely/Created in her sleep, this beauty in its centuries of wrong."

As the beauty sleeps, the reader awakens to Hesiod, who was "willing to do what nobody else would do," and to the idealized man, the Hero, fashioned out of dreamtime–"And your dream made him./He was yours and he was wise."—and the real joys and tragedies of love:

> "For fifteen years he never knew I never
> Came. The jerk. I faked, but anyone could have told.
> At last, 'Maybe it could be better,'
> I said. 'Why don't we go
> To one of those counselors?' and we did. Then after
> A spell we stopped. That was in '65. It's later
> Now. It's goddamn '75, and two years ago
> He 'came out,' as he called it, he went gay,
> And I'm—so soon, would you believe it?—I'm in menopause,
> And I don't feel so good,
> And no matter what, the diet, the exercise,
> I don't age nicely. Too much droop—
> Chin, breast, belly, ass. He said I should forget.
> And I said what the hell's the use. I sit on this stoop
> In the same old chair where grandmother used to set." (#42)

It is as much this dexterity with complicated images of relationship as his melopoeia that distinguishes the poetry of Hayden Carruth, and has for thirty years. This sorting through our own masculine and feminine aspects requires most of a lifetime of knowledgeable spirit, and, try as we might, we cannot forget what we have learned. Our tragedies are comic, our comedies all tragic:

> His name was Husband, his title Herr,
> noblest denomination, since he came from God
> In the olden tongue.
> ...
> He was Herr Husband,
> Householder, Handyman to all your joys,
> And if he stumbled or looked askance
> You had only to think your clever sexual thought
> That brought him to his parfit gentillesse again,
> Your knightly teacher whom none but you had taught. (#63)

The echoes and puns and allusions—Sylvia Plath to Chaucer—are no accident, but are a part of the whole resonance, the intellectual melopoeia of the poem, the "dance of the intellect" which inspires a need to speak. The poet's methods owe something to Pound's so-called "ideogrammic method," and to the Latin poets, Catullus and Lucretius.

Robert Duncan, in his essay, "Ideas of the Meaning of Form," quotes the closure of Williams's masterpiece "The Asphodel, That Greeny Flower," and then says, "The end of masterpieces ... the beginning of testimony. Having their mastery obedient to the play of forms that makes a path between what is in the language and what is in their lives. In this light that has something to do with all flowering things together, a free association of living things then – for my longing moves beyond governments to a co-operation; that may have seeds of being in free verse or free thought, or in that other free association where Freud led me to re-member (sic) their lives, admitting into the light of the acknowledged and then of meaning what had been sins and guilt, heresies, shames and wounds;/that may have to do with following the sentence along a line of feeling until the law becomes melody...."

Omnia, quae sunt, lumina sunt.

Or as Pound says in Canto 76: "nothing matters but the quality/of the affection – /in the end – that has carved the trace in the mind/dove sta memoria ..." Pound's own resonance is established by his quote from Guido Cavalcanti's "Donna Mi Prega," which recalls the hieratic triad Pound offers in his famous (and now largely unread) essay on Cavalcanti:

"memory   intelligence   will"

Pound being equally concerned with quality of affection which creates – *carves* – quality of memory. Identifying *qualitative* measures in "affection" is a very dangerous social undertaking, as any feminist must know; in a society built upon the exploitation of the Social Lie, it is truly revolutionary, threatening the very foundation of social structure. Carruth's poem is in every sense a feminist poem. After making love with a woman in his cabin – refusing to objectify her through graphic titillation – lying in an eternal moment,

> His being and hers were indistinguishable,
> So intermingled that he could not tell
> Which was man, which woman. Is that
> What Plato meant by the reunited
> Soul? Or his own sex-whelmed mind defecting?
> Neither hypothesis
> Appeals to him. He knows his feminine aspect,
> Always his, deeply and dearly his.
> He wonders: necessarily so are we all
> And why is it hidden? Without this synthesis
> How could we be, alone or together, whole? (#76)

He is filled with self-doubts and mistrusts even his own mind which may be defecting, telling him that his qualities of affection may be delusionary. But he also recognizes that only a complete synthesis of masculine and feminine within each of us can ever make us "whole" again. Two verses later, he thinks of classical women, "Helen, Julia, Amarintha," and others:

>   Julia had no wart? Or
> Cynthia no straggling yellow tooth?
> Then they were mere conceptions, youth
> Feminized, sexual but eternal, held
> In the long access of rhyme
> That you, dear dreamer, are inventing, romance unwilled
> And unrelenting.
>   And yet that time,
> He thinks, was actual: they lived, unknown women,
> Flawed and misnamed, their soft rank bodies prime
> For idealization. Convention is also human. (#78)

And still later, in another verse, "No love without hurt? No lovesong without distortion?/ ... We must love humanly, no debasement. We must sing/Our passion, as ineluctable as breath,/Without distortion, yet still this wondrous thing." Even in his rejection of most — not all, but most — of the conventions of the romantic tradition, Carruth makes a Romance.

Aristotle divided poetry into lyric, elegiac, epic, and dramatic; his categories were clearly conceived, and his organization is, at an elementary level, effective. But, much to the chagrin of our unifarcity departments of Literature, all such classification remains ultimately false. The drama, the epic, in Sophocles and Euripedes, unfolds — is spoken — in lyric lines. Even the concerns of the poetry itself defies classification as it seeks out truths as ancient as human knowledge. Near the end of *Philoktetes*, Sophocles has Neoptolemos tell Philoktetes, "And those who choose to clutch their miseries/and not release them deserve no pity./You have become a savage through your anger;/you refuse good advice and hate him who offers it."

Ugolino tells Dante in the midst of Hell, "Io no piangeva; si dentro inpietrai," or "Because I did not speak, I turned to stone inside." Hesiod believed that "Angels deliver light; the Muse delivers form."

Obeying the need to make music, the poem reveals itself in the act of being made. Carruth explores improvisation within a form in order to confront the demons of history that have traditionally punished woman for being woman, thereby separating masculine from feminine within each of us, and, by dividing rendering each impotent. The "meaning" of his long poem is inseparable from the sounds of the poem. All criticism, Eugenio Montale observes, is after the fact of the poem itself. The poet speaks from a deep need to *make music*. Valéry says somewhere, "An epic poem is a poem that can be told. When one tells it, one has a bilingual text." The poetry, of course, is *in the telling*. In verse 120, Carruth says,

> The border is what creates illegal aliens,
> Dividing what one knows from what one knows,
> This called an "imaginary line,"
> Not even drawn on the snow,
> With a huge officious multilingual sign ...
> Action and knowledge are one, free, far in the depths of
>   consciousness.

It is not the poet's intention to cross borders, but to demolish them. And by the 124th chorus, he tells his awakening Beauty,

> The sun
> Will rise on the snowy firs and set on the sleeping
> Lavender mountain as always, and no one

> Will possess or command or defile you where you belong,
> Here in the authentic world.
>   The work is done.
> My name is Hayden and I have made this song.

Beginning his song with a loose pentameter, and having played in and with its tenets and variations for one hundred and twenty-four choruses, all but one restricted to fifteen lines, he closes his poem on a pentameter. It is a song which includes resonances from history and philosophy, literature, music (especially jazz), The Arts—but not as though they were different things. Nor are they more or less important than the "nine little birds" of chorus 27. They are resonances, which are what music is, their sounds are heard clearly by those who have learned to listen, by the knowledgeable spirit.

    The Sleeping Beauty is perhaps Hayden Carruth's grandest achievement. It is astonishingly inclusive, making use of his enormous narrative skills as in *Brothers, I Loved You All,* formal without being awkward or self-conscious, lyrical in its execution and epic in its proportion, sweeping in its broad affections and horrors. Squarely in the American romantic-mythopoeic tradition, *The Sleeping Beauty* is a sustained visionary icon of our culture. It returns to us a spirit now too often missing in our poetry, one which dares the sustained experience, a spirit which encourages as many literary lions as housecats. There was a time when we still believed in classics—not only the ancient classics, but the modern and the contemporary as well—no matter that the list was and is constantly changing. In such a circumstance, *The Sleeping Beauty* is a classic. And because it is a contemporary classic written in the purr and roar of a lion, it has been read almost exclusively by Carruth's fellow poets. It is time for a little lyrical genius to trickle down into the economy of our communal souls.

O the thought of what America would be like if the classics had a wide circulation!

William Matthews

The Poetry Blues

"The truth is," Hayden Carruth writes in a concluding sentence to one of the essays in *Sitting In: Selected Writings on Jazz, Blues, and Related Topics* (University of Iowa Press, 1986), "whether for good or ill and to the extent — is it any at all? — that we enjoy freedom of choice in this world, poetry for me was, and is, second-best to jazz."

"To my mind Schopenhauer was right when he suggested that the other arts aspire to the condition of music," Carruth writes in another essay, "except that I wish he had said 'ought to aspire.'" And elsewhere he quotes Nietzsche: "Without music life would be a mistake."

In "Mystery and Expressiveness," Carruth describes a talk he has given several times. He plays a blues by Billie Holiday.

> At the end is a one-bar tag by [Ben] Webster on tenor, and at the very end, just after the final beat but while the tone is still sounding, somebody moans. It is scarcely audible, but in my talk I play the final bars again with the volume turned up so that the audience can hear it easily ... Then I ask the audience what this moan means.

The impossibility of an exact answer to this question is what makes music so hard to write about and, interestingly enough, is exactly what makes the enterprise so precious to Carruth.

"Got Those Forever Inadequate Blues," another essay is called, and in it Carruth writes that

> [I] can never arrive at a linguistic formulation of the musical expressiveness of the blues. The best I have been able to do so far is to say that it is a sensual experience of seeking and failing, that is, of inadequacy.

The blues may be "the musical expression of existentialist thought and feeling," as Carruth goes on to say, but I doubt it. In this formulation, the urge of prose argument to elicit agreement from a reader has replaced something direct and impervious to reason that is the source of music's power. Music can persuade without soliciting consent, and that's what Carruth, and any poet in his or her right mind, envies. Orpheus was a musician.

Carruth is one those poets for whom the inexpressible and the unspeakable are the best ambitions of language, so that writing is necessarily an experience of seeking and failing. We're near a working definition of desire, if desire is understood to be a longing whose most likely capture is itself.

It's not that music is *about* desire; that moan can't be readily translated into language. It's that the love of music recapitulates desire. Carruth is not only a listener but has also been a player, and what musician—even, and perhaps especially even, the very finest—hasn't felt, in the gap between what he can hear in his head and what he can play on his instrument, a figure for human longing and imperfection? There are nights it feels like *the* figure for human longing and imperfection.

Jazz, blues *and* related topics, *Sitting In*'s subtitle promises. There are twenty-five essays interleaved by thirteen poems.

The best of these poems, "Freedom and Discipline," is Carruth's version of Dryden's "Ode on St. Cecilia's Day."

> Saint Harmony, many
> years I have stript
>
> naked in your service
> under the lash. Yes, …

Carruth begins with the combination of penitence and eroticism that is the central tone of this remarkable book. "Freedom and discipline concur/only in ecstasy," the poem finds a way to assert near its end, and the religious and sexual meanings of discipline and ecstasy are braided to identity.

Carruth includes literary essays on Tom McGrath and on *Middlemarch* that benefit wonderfully from their new context.

What kind of a novel is *Middlemarch*, he asks? Not a psychological novel, not a novel of manners, not a philosophical novel. "In fact not one principal is an interesting person." It is instead, Carruth decides, "a meditative lyric in prose that uses … contrived anecdote to explore the failure of mankind in relation to [marriage]." It doesn't fit received categories of expectation and response but compels a powerful reaction, so what is it? An embodiment of longing. A book about seeking and failing.

Carruth sees McGrath's work as misunderstood and underloved because it, too, falls outside our learned habits of reading. McGrath's body of work is sprawled and uneven, but the examples Carruth gives are commandingly beautiful.

Less well received by the context are a review of James Wright's *Collected Prose* and an appreciation of Robert Duncan, but they're interesting in themselves. Carruth could write as a learned critic if he wanted to, but his manner is more like Virginia Woolf's or Randall Jarrell's; he writes as a reader who happens to be a writer.

Except he has nearly a theory, actually a set of variations on an unstated and inexpressible theme; though *theme* is the wrong word for the moan that ends the Billie Holiday blues.

"I am not a musicologist, but a poet," Carruth says in a footnote, but his essays "The Blues Scale" and "Influences: The Formal Idea of Jazz" are theoretically sound; he knows his stuff.

But he prefers "technical criticism" (e.g., Gunther Schuller's *Early Jazz*) to "impressionistic writing, … the kind of thing done by Whitney Balliett, … [which] exploits the reader by promising what it cannot deliver, an explanation or at least a description of the expressiveness of jazz, which every fully engaged listener longs for."

Schuller's work is exacting but his prose turgid. Balliett can write with grace and a fidelity to his own listening experience that has nothing to do with the slur in "impressionistic," which implies that our sensory grasp of music is not the beginning of the urge to music criticism but somehow an impediment to it.

The problem is, as Carruth insists throughout, that what jazz expresses is otherwise inexpressible. That's why the collective invention of jazz is so important: it expands our range of access to our emotions. That we can't explain how this works in discursive prose reminds us how much we needed jazz, and shouldn't be, for poets, a first instance of the limits of discursive prose.

As Carruth says, the blues scale cannot be objectively notated.

"It is subjective. It is an understanding that is felt. Is this a monstrous obstacle? Not at all. The understanding can be transmitted by the simplest means, i.e., from ear to ear."

What kind of understanding is this?

In "The Guy Downstairs," Carruth describes sitting down with the pianist Don Ewell, in Ewell's flat, to play (clarinet is Carruth's instrument), and after the first few bars the guy downstairs would start to beat on the ceiling with a broomhandle. "Sometimes he did it so quickly it seemed as if he must have been waiting there for us to begin." When it seems as if "the guy downstairs has taken over the world," when one feels an outsider, jazz and blues can express it, and, even better, they contain the paradoxical knowledge that it is actually what seems most to isolate us from others, our shame, our solitude, our truculence, that is most human in us. And they give it voice.

Some of the understanding is about love. "The main thing, in jazz as in all the arts, is first to care, then to know, and finally to appreciate, i.e., to avoid and combat musicology and other such forms of pedantic historicism like the plague. To this main thing I have given a large part of my life, and I am glad of it."

Some of the understanding is about mixed feelings. Carruth is here, as in his poems, willing to be intellectually inconsistent, as in the case of technical critcism and musicology, because there's emotional truth in that ambivalence.

And there's real understanding available about race in American life. Performed or recorded jazz of course belongs to any listener who will meet it. But white people couldn't have invented jazz and there was little in white American culture to suggest to us how badly we needed it. Carruth writes well on this topic, which has undone so many jazz writers. He's resistant to sweeping theories of all sorts, and this helps him. And of course he can hear in the music itself a kind of racial subplot, a "story," in the sense that early jazz musicians used the word to denote a solo that went somewhere rather than diddling in place. Part of that story is much of what most white Americans know about what it might be like to be black.

And part of that story is a visionary dream of "a great session where race has no significance at all ... [and] every performer and listener participates freely and equally in the bodily and spiritually wrenching, exhilarating, purging experience of jazz-in-itself." It's with this dream that Carruth ends the last essay in his book:

"I dream the dream that I thought was an actuality when I was a boy. It cannot happen. But may we not go in that direction?" The best answer to that question is probably the moan at the end of the Billie Holiday blues.

Geoffrey Gardner

Homage to the One-Man Band with Incredible Ears

In little more than the last eight years, Hayden Carruth has published three books of collected essays and five new books of poetry. They are the exhibits of an astonishing abundance, not just in their quality, but in their variety, their urgency and clarity. In tension with his intrinsic Yankee reticence, Carruth's poetry has always been deeply personal, intimate not only in tone but also candidly self-revealing. Yet even at his most personal, Carruth has opened his poetry and allowed it to be full of many other people and the multiplicity of their relations. He has let go the pursuit of a personal mythology for the creation of a personal world. Making the usual allowances for differences of temperament, local detail, insight and outlook, it is very much the world we all inhabit.

Carruth is a cosmopolitan of the sticks and the peripheries whose vision has been magnified, not reduced, by his dislocation from the geographical centers. This stands to reason. For all of us, locally rooted as we may be, it is the totality of the fumbling great world – this floating empire of gigantism and destruction whose circumferences are everywhere and whose center, on close inspection, appears to be Nowhere – that really is our only home. All this is to say that Carruth is a localist who has striven to become a poet of world consciousness. He has succeeded in this by recognizing that the so-called existential dilemma is identical to the age-old and worldwide human plight, the morality play of unforeknown climax now playing itself out, not only in our newspapers, but in the real lives of real people, all of us, you and me.

Carruth's most recent book of poetry, whose almost freakishly odd title is *Tell Me Again How the White Heron Rises and Flies Across the Nacreous River at Twilight Toward the Distant Islands,* falls somewhere between the loose organization of his miscellaneous collections and the intensely idiosyncratic unity of his booklength poems. What draws the poems in *Heron* so closely together is Carruth's relentless concentration on a single group of themes, the occasions that give rise to them as well as the thoughts and feelings that emanate from them and their mutual interlocking. The themes are big ones: love and death, poetry and exile.

Almost ten years ago, I wrote and published a long essay on Carruth's poetry. I tried to cram it as full as I could of good sense and passionate praise because Carruth's poems—as much as any others—had helped to sustain my life and feed my understanding of our experience of the world. A lot of the river runs past one's door in ten years, cutting a channel one hopes is deeper and not just inevitably narrower. But I would not tinker now with a single sentence of what I wrote about Carruth's poetry ten years ago. It remains the adequate record I could manage then of what Carruth's poems are striving for and a true tracing of where I had been in relation to them. Still, there is one sentence in that essay that touches on the matter of exile and gives me pause. I wrote, "... discipline granted Carruth the gift of that true spontaneity which is the ability to refuse alienation for the sake of a life and power of vision wedded by necessity to the world." That, I'm afraid, sounds as if I meant that poetic discipline, and the spontaneity it yields, freed Carruth, and could free anyone, from the universal condition of alienation in some final way. It's simply not so. The evidence all goes the other way. Virtually every poem in *Heron*, as well as most everything else Carruth has written, begins with or reverts to the experience of exile or grapples with the problem of alienation. "To refuse alienation" is not to deny it or pretend it does not exist, but to stand against it in defiance, even in defiance of intelligent good sense, with all the effort of imaginative will one is capable of.

Unrestrained commerce, technology and political power, to one degree or another, drive all of us from home. They divide the workman from his tools and his products, the artist and the scholar from their audiences, the teacher from his pupils, children from their parents, lovers from each other and all of us from our senses. To one degree or another, we are all displaced persons, enduring our towns and cities, whether they are shiny or shabby, as if they were refugee camps where the centers of communication treat us all like cultured fungoids, keeping us in the dark and feeding us manure. In poetry and prose, Carruth has written of all this frequently and well, with compassion and a rebel's insight. It is very much the background out of which the many characters of *Asphalt Georgics* emerge to say their say.

But Carruth is no kind of party man or political propagandist. As a poet he has inquired beyond politics into the ecology of human consciousness and action to probe the points of failing balance and disequilibrium that historically have driven us to foul and destroy our own roosts and nests and in the present moment are propelling us to threaten not only the continuation of our own nature and its fate but the survival of nature as such. And this is very much the subject of his anti-romantic contribution to the tradition of romantic poetry, *The Sleeping Beauty*.

But in Carruth's best and most personal poems, there has always also been the deeper vision of existence itself as chaotic and unmeaning mutability, the source of exile and universal homesickness, of desperation and sadness, "this saturation of everything, this seepage into the world." Through all the poems of *Heron*, this ultimate sense of the negative aspects of Being is never far from the surface. In "Ovid Old Buddy, I would Discourse with You a While," Carruth identifies his exile in Syracuse, N.Y., with Ovid's on the Thracian shore as the latter looks "blankly out to the rocks and the gray ocean," writing his letter forever to Tiberius to "obtain your pardon, your freedom to return/to Rome, so long denied by Augustus." Ovid writes his letter forever, but Carruth says that Ovid like all of us is trapped in "that instant of mutability continuing forever/between a death and an investiture," and there is no pardon. From that follows our sadness and our desperation. In "Cross My Heart and Hope to Die, It Was the Very Same Song Exactly," Carruth further names the sadness as "the mystery of beginning, a parchment map with terra incognita/Inscribed on the northeastern sector." Disorientation and the pain of longing for home are the consequences of being set free in a universe of existence where the mind cannot discover landmarks for itself.

In the long and overwhelming elegy for his mother that closes

Heron, Carruth writes of his mother crying out from the agony of her deathbed and her damaged soul, "O Hayden, take me home," but in her aphasia she mistakes her home for England. The agony of her dying lasts,

> Three years. For you they could have been three million.
> You live only
> In the present moment,
> The moment before death.

Aphasic, suffering, "smashed, a machine of random parts, of no definable function," Carruth's mother lies "on the shore of death, perpetually," "peering into the darkness" and enduring the endless moment between death and the divestment of all ability to make sense or take comfort. Hers is the condition of Ovid, stripped of his forlorn power of formulation and of hope.

When at last she dies, Carruth performs in imagination a bridal ritual of rejoicing for her departure on the sea of death, "For the passage out of consciousness is at least in itself a minor advantage,/ Though it is not a passage out of existence." And here he concludes by saying: "To rejoice for death is to mourn existence,/... as animals who regard the world with scorn." The world merits this "proud resentment" because, "Existence is the crime against the existing." Like Carruth's mother, victims of our own innocence, and penitent for the crimes committed against us, we all are, "Drifting, drifting in the uncaused universe that has no right to be." Finally, the absolute, impenetrable and unbreakable mystery is death. It can be revealed but only as total inexplicability. And still we must mourn and reconcile ourselves to it and stand against it in defiance.

But as ever, for Carruth there are experiences and markings in the world that enjoin "our otherwise denatured sensibilities to perceive and understand the positive apects of Being." If existence is uncaused and random contingency, its other face is the current of total freedom, "The continuum of what really is, what only is" that is always there if we can awake to it. At times in the poems in *Heron*, Carruth refers to it abstractly as "The Absolute," attainable by imagination, "this letting power ... the one absolution." But "out/here in the garden of sensational thought," it takes many forms: the sound of the wind in the chimney that says, "finitude, finitude" or "the complex discourse about something/Altogether mysterious" of the migrating geese that Carruth and his lover hear while lying in bed. It is the meaning Being intimates just beyond the grasp of mind and which calls for our response, "though we cannot/ Articulate it." But it also appears in these lines, ending a poem called "Sometimes When Lovers Lie Quietly Together, Unexpectedly One of Them Will Feel the Other's Pulse":

> Above the street at heavy opalescent noontime two electrical
>   cables, strung from pole to pole,
> Hung in relationship to one another such that the lower swung
>   in and out of the shadow of the one above it,
> And as it did so the sunlight reflected from it was sprung
>   gleaming outward and inward along its length,
> A steady expansion and contradiction. And for a while I was
>   taken away from my discontents
> By this rhythm of the truth of the world, so fundamental, so
>   simple, so clear.

The continuum of Being as freedom is the source of

>   ... the
> joy, beyond ego, be-
> yond the fracturing
> stones of the objective
> world, the strata, the
> massive tablets of
> God ...
>   ... I
> compose, therefore I
> am not.

This continuum is the ground of a transcendence that does not deny but subsumes and transforms the sorrow of Being, often through the freedom of song, at best in the music of the jazz musicians to whom Carruth so frequently recurs:

> The old, old pattern of call and response unending,
> And they felt the stir of the animal's soul in the cave,
> And heard the animal's song,

>   Indefinable utterance, and saw
>   A hot flowing of the eternal, many-colored, essential plasm
>   As they leaned outward together, away from place, from time,
>   In one only person, which was the blues.

I don't want to involve either myself or the reader in a technical discussion of the mastery of Carruth's verse. Rather by quoting this much of it, I hope that mastery will be evident to all who take the trouble to read aloud what I have quoted. Throughout all of Carruth's best poetry there is a pervasive music, sometimes eerie, sometimes ferocious, and at times sweet in its meditations. This music is the product of the dramatic energy of any person's fall from plus to minus and his rise again to plus. It is also identical in its formation to the quality of the sublime so often present in Carruth's best work. By "the sublime," I simply mean the reaching of the mind to comprehend what is beyond all our categories of understanding. And by "the mind," I mean no more nor less than the whole person in his multifarious relations to others and the world. The effort of the mind to encompass the positive and negative aspects of Being in one synoptic view can bring the comic mask into superimposition upon the tragic one. I think this is the origin of the curious, almost mocking, irony of many of the titles of poems in *Heron*. It is the spring that gives rise to the strange humor that appears in some of Carruth's poems, for example in "Underground the Darkness Is the Light." It is a kind of quietly maniacal hilarity that often has reminded me of the energy and laughter of Melville, that other great Yankee anatomist of good and evil.

Carruth has often written that between the poles of freedom and discipline he has sought ecstasy as the resolution of desperation through song. More than once, he has said that had he been given the choice, he would have spent his life playing the blues in some corner of New York with Sid Catlett, Vic Dickenson, Benny Carter and the rest, but lacking that choice poetry has always been for him second-best to jazz. Well, maybe so. I certainly can understand this as Carruth's protest at being deprived of the special satisfactions of jazz, which are communal, and being stuck instead with poetry, which is a creature of solitude. As a poet, Carruth himself has been a most incredible one-man band with wonderful ears. Yet, though poetry arises in solitude – that word much abused by our overuse of it – it is not about isolation. It may emerge from "the unrelenting/ awareness of being our own future/in the mode of not-being."

But further back, it begins in the person's contact with the other and strives forward to reach the other again. *Heron* includes a group of poems where Carruth meditates on the function of the poet and on the nature of poetry. In "The Necessary Impresario, Mr. Septic Tanck," Carruth reintroduces a character who first told his story in *Asphalt Georgics*. There he said:

> ... Septic Tanck is a real good shook-
> down name for a poet nowadays, the
> ending-up place for everything, don't you
> know, everything that comes down.

Here, in *Heron*, he identifies the poem as "a leak in the cranium." This view of the poet as scapegoat-*cum*-cultural-waste-disposal-system recalls to me Joyce's bitter poem, "The Holy Office," where the poet, Katharsis-Purgative, gleefully accepts that others

> Make me the sewer of their clique.
> That they may dream their dreamy dreams
> I carry off their filthy streams.

But Carruth, fortunately, is nowhere near that bitter. He parodies Wallace Stevens ("The house was quiet and the night was irrelevant") and chides him because poetry "was not a moral question with him, however/It ought to have been." But he also thanks Stevens and concludes that, "The poem is always something one slips under/ Somebody's door/... a present for which we invent birthdays/Right and left." Carruth rejects both of the dominant and endlessly contending views of our culture that a poem is either an expression or an object. Rather it "is for us what instinct is for animals, a continuing and chiefly unthought corroboration of essence." But more still than that, it is most urgently and vitally "a gift, a bestowal." It is, like a kiss, an act of love, a "paradigm of fecundity."

That word, "bestowal," is an important one. To bestow is not only to confer as a gift, but to offer in marriage, to use, and, at bottom, to house. The poem, then, is both a shelter from the storms of Being and the storehouse for the positive aspects of Being. In another poem, Carruth says, "that freedom is from the world and found in the technology of building/... But is not the technology of the brickmakers and bricklayers/what captures for us the song of the wind?" And, remember, the song of the wind in the chimney is "finitude, finitude."

In "Survival as Tao, Beginning at 5:00 A.M.," art and love begin to merge more closely. The poem, he says, is an act of love. Carruth risks two daring formulations:

> ... Music is the attempt to survive the unbearable through
>   freedom from objectivity
> Bestowed from the outside, *i.e.*, by the variable frequencies
>   of sound waves.

And:

> ... Loving Cindy is to survive the unbearable through freedom
>   bestowed
> From the inside, mutually.

Finally, he concludes by saying:

> ... in the freedom of orgasm my thoughts of her
> Are indeed a song, a metaphysical song, a soaring in the
>   inconceivable, brought to the fullness of harmony
> By her thoughts of me.

I hope these lines show plainly enough Carruth's tendency to aphorisms that matter, what Kenneth Burke used to call "equipment for living." And what a splendid thing it is to have breathing among us a poet who risks making formulations that move the heart and stir the mind from its all too customary torpor.

But both poems and love are themselves problematical and engender problems of gratitude and adequacy and of the consonance of life with spirit. Part of the moral meaning of Carruth's poetry is that in the end—that is, here at the end—love is more important and more necessary than poetry, for the problems of both

> ... have no solutions
> except when we wash them away on
>
> salty tides of loving as we rock in
> the dark sure sea of our existence.

    This imagery of the sea is also worth noting. It is strange to find it present so frequently in the imagination of a landlocked poet. It is "the dark sure sea of our existence," but it is also the home of the great tortoise whose eyes are filmed with the tears of the sadness of the world. It appears as the sea-surge that holds Carruth's mind as he reads his friend's poems of aging and death and which comes back to him as the seething of the traffic on the interstate as he walks in the woods and broods on those poems. It is the sea that separates Ovid in his exile from home. The sea is both "the flow of motherhood" from which we all emerge and the current that carries Carruth's mother into death in the boat of her confinement. The sea is comfort and risk. Grasping, we mistake the threads of spume for straws and go under. But if we give ourselves to the wave, we displace no more than our own bodies' weight of water and are carried ... maybe to shore, maybe further out to sea. And in place of grasping, it is possible to risk by resting "our hands in a lovers' clasp," sheltering the spark of the community of love, the only community that is and is worthy of our belonging.

    Carruth is more than a good poet. He is one of the responsible laborers who has set his work against the tides and washes of suffering. For that I thank him and salute him and wish him long years and much joy.

Carolyn Kizer

Others Call It God

In the early sixties, when I was editing *Poetry Northwest*, I received a group of poems from Hayden Carruth, including a sonnet called, "Ontological Episode of the Asylum." Although I had read a number of his poems and some of his criticism with admiration, I did not know Carruth personally. But this group of poems was the beginning of a friendship which has remained steadfast ever since. The sonnet, in particular, moved me then — to the point where I almost instantly memorized it — and moves me now, not only because the form is perfectly subsumed in the subject but because it summed up my own feelings about belief:

> The boobyhatch's bars, the guards, the nurses,
> The illimitable locks and keys are all arranged
> To thwart the hand that continually rehearses
> Its ending stroke and raise a barricade
> Against destruction-seeking resolution.
> Many of us in there would have given all
> (But we had nothing) for one small razor blade
> Or seventy grams of the comforting amytal.
>
> So I went down in the attitude of prayer,
> Yes, to my knees on the cold floor of my cell,
> Humped in a corner, a bird with a broken wing,
> And asked and asked as fervently and well
> As I could guess to do for light in the mists
> Of death, until I learned God doesn't care.
> Not only that, he doesn't care at all,
> One way or the other. That is why he exists.

I am surely not the only person to be reminded of the famous passage in William James's *The Varieties of Religious Experience*, where he speaks in the guise of a Frenchman "in a bad nervous condition." Later, he confessed that this had been his own experience:

> While in this state of philosophic pessimism and general depression of spirits about my prospects, I went one evening into a dressing-room in the twilight to procure some article that was there; when suddenly there fell upon me without warning, just as if it came out of the darkness, a horrible fear of my own exis-

tence. Simultaneously there arose in my mind the image of an epileptic patient whom I had seen in the asylum, a black-haired youth with greenish skin, entirely idiotic, who used to sit all day on one of the benches, or rather shelves against the wall, with his knees drawn up against his chin .... This image and my fear entered into a species of combination with each other. *That shape am I,* I felt, potentially. Nothing that I possess can defend me against that fate, if the hour for it should strike for me as it struck for him ... I have always thought that this experience of melancholia of mine had a religious bearing.

On responding to a question of himself by himself, James added, "I mean that the fear was so invasive and powerful that if I had not clung to scripture—texts like 'The eternal God is my refuge,' etc., 'Come unto me, all ye that labor and are heavy laden,' etc., I think I should have grown really insane."

Of course calling on God in extremis is not unique to poet and philosophers, but to pray without any expectation of being heard or being helped is perhaps more unusual. It could even be considered an act of heroism, as indeed Carruth calls it in another poem, "Once and Again," written more than a dozen years later, in a situation similar to that of the sonnet:

> To believe in the God
> who does not exist is a heroism of faith, much needed in these times,
> I agree, I know, especially since the hero is and must always be
> unrecognized. But to love the God that does not exist, to love
>   the love
> that does not exist, this is more than heroism, it is perhaps almost
> saintliness, such as we can know it. To discover and to hold, to
>   resurrect
> an idea for its own sake ...

To me, Carruth exaggerates the element of heroism and "perhaps almost saintliness" in this gratuitous love of God, and underestimates the neurotic/creative act of the imagination which makes it possible. Elsewhere in *The Varieties of Religious Experience,* James makes the point that, "Few of us are not in some ways infirm, or even diseased; and our very infirmities help us unexpectedly." "If there were such a thing as inspiration from a higher realm, it might well be that the neurotic temperament would furnish the chief condition of the requisite receptivity." From the pit of our desperation we call out to God, even if we don't believe in him, and in the state of receptivity engendered by fear, particularly fear of the cosmos, we may even dream of a response, although not a personal one, and not a comforting one. The sole comfort comes from the act of prayer itself.

Later, James quotes Sabatier, the "liberal French theologian," perhaps the inspiration for James's imaginary Frenchman, in regard to prayer: "Religion is nothing if it be not the vital act by which the entire mind seeks to save itself by clinging to the principle from which it draws its life. This act is prayer, by which term I understand no vain exercise of words, no mere repetition of certain sacred formulae, but the very movement itself of the soul.... Wherever the interior prayer is lacking, there is no religion; wherever, on the other hand, the prayer rises and stirs the soul, even in the absence of forms or doctrines, we have living religion." Sabatier, however, would not agree with Carruth because he believed that prayer was a putting of one's self into a personal relation with a mysterious power, while the prayers of unbelieving believers go out to an indifferent God, a God who may not exist at all except as we pray to It.

At the end of his book, James remarks that the God whom science recognizes "must be a God of universal laws exclusively, a God who does a wholesale, not a retail business. He cannot accommodate his processes to the convenience of individuals." "Convenience" is perhaps too casual a word to describe the emotions of those who, in primal panic, fall on their knees in the desperate hope that God will respond and save. Carruth is harsh in his response to John Berryman's late conversion to belief in a personal God, Berryman, too, an alcoholic and — to use Carruth's own word about himself —"crazy." For most of his life Berryman had believed in a transcendent God —"a formal principle of sorts holding the vast complicated harmony of the universe together." This view is rather like the speculative theology of Empedocles, who spoke of God as "a sacred and unutterable mind, flashing through the whole world with rapid thought." Near his end, in the sixth of his "Eleven Addresses to the Lord," Berryman began:

> Under new management, Your majesty:
> Thine. I have solo'd mine since childhood, since
> my father's suicide when I was twelve
> blew out my most bright candle faith, and look at me ...
>
> My double nature fused in that point of time
> three weeks ago day before yesterday.
> Now, brooding thro' a history of the early Church
> I identify with everybody, even the heresiarchs.

Carruth was infuriated with the precise dating of Berryman's revelation, and refused to believe "this boasting, equivocating secularist," when he reviewed *Love & Fame* in *The Nation*. (Are we least sympathetic with those who share some of our darkest failings?)

Perhaps we might agree with one of James's critics who said that "his need to believe was tantamount to having faith" (but this is an attempt to clarify what James deliberately chose to keep obscure). Or, if we cannot agree, we may at least sympathise with those who feel that, in order to stave off insanity, they require some form of belief. Carruth goes out of his way to deny his own belief, but all the same he turns to God when he is "crazy" and only then.

The following is from "The Bloomingdale Papers," the poems of his craziness, published after the fact in 1975:

> Save me, O God; for the waters are come in
>   unto my soul.
>
> I sink in deep mire, where there is no standing:
> I am come into deep waters, where the floods
>   overflow me.
> I am weary of my crying: my throat is dried:
>   mine eyes fail ...
>
> Deliver me out of the mire, and let me not sink:
> let me be delivered from them that hate me,
> and out of the deep waters.

> Let not the waterflood overflow me, neither
> let the deep swallow me up,
> and let not the pit
> shut her mouth upon me.
>
> (Carruth's own version of the
> 69th Psalm, verses 1–3, 14–16)

In a review in *Harper's* in 1976, Carruth says that "the answer to grief is God, but God does not answer." What then are we to make of his denial of belief coupled with his cries to cold heaven?

In an essay called "Who I Am, 1" he says, speaking of critics, that "they will not consider the work of art as *a transaction between the artist's soul and God* — substitute whatever other two words you like. But that's what it is." (My italics.) I think we must focus on the artist negotiating with his angel — his muse — rather than simply as a man pleading with God, as in the chant of the psalmist quoted above.

In another essay called "The Act of Love: Poetry and Personality," also published in 1976, Carruth restates a position he had taken earlier, in an essay on Robert Lowell: "The poet," he says, "was engaged in the conversion of crude experience into personality through metaphor and the other disciplines of the instrumental imagination," using the term "personality" to mean "the whole individual subjectivity, the spirit-body-soul."

I'm not entirely happy with Carruth's use of the term personality (in fact when I first typed the title of this essay I freudianly left off half of it: Poetry and Personality). Of course we are in semantic difficulties, as is almost invariably the case when attempting to talk of matters spiritual and metaphysical. There is no dictionary of personality which includes the entity spirit-body-soul, but it's a question of who is master here, and in this case we must concede that Carruth is. But he does seem to leave out a vital step, *the* vital step of the process, which is the conversion of crude experience into the final product, which is art. I find that a great deal of the poetry being written today is hung up on precisely that hook: personality, whether interpreted narrowly or in the broadest sense; and that the act of transcendence never takes place because the personality intervenes.

But let us go along with Carruth as he expands his definition. He says, further, that personality is universal and relative; it exists in every consciousness. "Personality is a phenomenon of pure existence and occurs in what have been called our existential moments, our moments outside time." The existential moment for the poet occurs when she or he is "intensely engaged in a poem, spontaneously engendering imagery and verbal compounds from the imaginative structures of remembered experience.... It is a spiritual happening — at least I do not know what else to call it." Nor do I.

Carruth asserts again that he is not a religious person. He cannot "project this concept of spirit and personality onto any traditional religion that I know, although analogues and affinities occur in many of them." Further, he says that he uses the word "spiritual" to mean "the substance of feeling when personality passes out of time's determinants and into pure essence, which I have called eternity; and in poems I have spoken of meetings there with the holy spirit, though my meaning has not been the same one that Christians use when they refer to the third attribute of the Trinity." "Chiefly I think of the transcendence of personality as a process of innerness, and of the holy spirit as my own." (My own preference would be to use "identity," even spiritual identity, rather than personality. Moreover, I don't see how Carruth can call the holy spirit "my own" when he has supposedly transcended his personality.)

But by now I believe that we have circled back to where we started: with Carruth's poems. In his shying away from the thought that he is a religious man, or a man who can relate to a form of traditional religion, he is in a sense contradicting his own poems, which seem to tell a different story. How many of these defiant rejections of any whiff of traditional faith might have been rendered unnecessary — and conserving of psychic energy — if we, like the American Indians before us, believed in and called upon The Great Spirit, rather than God!

Poetry is not prayer, but it is not not prayer. Prayer is not often poetry, but the greatest prayers are poems. To me, the spiritual is the spiritual, no matter how we quibble over terminology, qualify it or attempt to redefine it. Spirituality is identical with, and achieved through, an act of love. Carruth says as much at the close of his essay: "What I have in mind is what has been called in other places the 'aesthetic emotion,' the feeling that overlies substance and converts substance, whether beautiful or ugly, into something else. Sometimes this 'something else' has been called beauty, but the term is likely to be misunderstood" (like all other terms we have been using). "I prefer to call it spiritual love, the state of being of a pure existence, and the aesthetic emotion is the experience of that state."

However, none of these aesthetic impulses, no matter what their degree of spirituality, can succeed in warding off that cosmic fear. When, in the night, it overtakes us, we turn instinctively to prayer, to the great spirit who is within us. As for me, I pray a good deal, even when I'm not scared or miserable. And one of the people I pray for, nearly every day, is my dear friend, Hayden Carruth. God may not listen or care, one way or the other. But it exists.

David Budbill

When You Use Your Head, Your Ears Fall Off: My Twenty Years of Listening to Music with the Supernumerary Cockroach

I

Again and again when I go to somebody's house they say, "Hey! I got this great new album I want you to hear." So they put the record on and not eight bars into the first cut they start talking and then everybody starts talking and the party is on. And, once again, the music becomes what it almost always is in our lives, background something-or-other for that jawing noise we make with our mouths and throats and tongues. When the record is over somebody *might* say, "Man, isn't that great?" And somebody else might say, "Oh, yeah, that was fantastic." Although usually nobody says anything, they just keep talking because nobody has even noticed that the music stopped.

In the world of music when somebody says you have "good ears" it means you play well by ear, you articulate on your instrument what you hear being played, either outside yourself by others or, more mysteriously, inside yourself, by those inner musicians, inner voices, who/which are always calling to any artist from the other world, the other side.

Over the music stand in the corner of my writing room where I practice my saxophone, I have a sign, a little piece of advice I made up to give myself, which says:

> WHEN YOU USE YOUR HEAD
> YOUR EARS FALL OFF.
> DON'T THINK:
> LISTEN

In other words, if I try to *think* my way through the chord changes on which a particular tune is constructed, if I try to *think up* my musical poem, I can't play. However, if I relax and *listen* carefully and accurately enough to that other melody, the one I can hear being played inside me, then I can play, and it is likely to sound pretty good. If I put thinking in the place of listening, my "good ears" fall off.

II

For the past twenty years Hayden Carruth has been for me a hawk-eyed critic and a steadfast friend. Over those years together we have been through myriad personal traumas in both our lives, shared many mutual loves and hates, pleasures and consternations. And through all this we have spent almost all of our time together not talking about literature or gossiping about fellow writers, in fact, not talking at all, but listening instead to music. What we have shared most and most deeply over the years is our mutual love for the music invented by African Americans, the music some people call jazz.

I want to say here, although it seems almost ridiculous to have to say it, that when Hayden and I listen to music together, we listen. We don't talk while the music is playing, we talk after the music stops. Music is a conversation in another language; it is someone speaking directly to you, and, as your mother must have told you, it is impolite to talk while someone else is speaking.

We've spent twenty years listening together and when we are not together, which is most of the time, we send tapes back and forth and then talk and write to each other about what we hear. I want to remember here four specific times out of those twenty years of listening together.

First. Twenty years ago. I was just getting to know Hayden. I was at his little house on Clay Hill, a mile or so northwest of Johnson, Vermont, the little house that stood beside what seemed to me the always roaring brook. We were in his tiny living/dining room, I standing beside the brown, sheet-metal kerosene pot burner that heated the main part of the house. Hayden said, "Listen to this," and he put on to his old and rickety portable record player a cut from a record made live at the 1959 Belgium World's Fair Jazz Festival. The players were Sidney Bechet on soprano sax, Buck Clayton on trumpet, Vic Dickenson on trombone and a rhythm section neither one of us can remember. Actually, I couldn't remember any of these details, but, typically, when I asked Hayden, he could.

It was a blues, called simply, "Society Blues," one of those names thought up in a second and stuck onto a tune to give it a name for the album, an impromptu blues of numerous choruses over basic changes, a chance for each soloist to have his say, at least this is the way I remember it. And when it came Vic Dickenson's turn, he had plenty to say! He launched into his solo and proceeded to utter one of the most scathing bits of social commentary I have ever heard – or read. He played the ugliest, nastiest, meanest, most sarcastic, most biting, most hilarious series of ... let Hayden say it as he said it of another time when Vic Dickenson let loose:

> Smears, brays – Christ
>   the dirtiest noise imaginable
>   belches, farts
>   *curses*
>   but it was music

In other words, how else is a Black man lost in a racist society to have his say and still keep his neck the length it is supposed to be? Defiance. Defiance. Vic Dickenson had articulated an essential element in the music of blues and jazz: defiance.

Last year I had a conversation with saxophonist David Murray in which we were both bemoaning the state of lifelessness and conservatism that has swept through not only poetry and jazz but all the arts. I remember at one point Murray saying, "When I was coming up we just naturally felt it was important to defy."

Second. Ten years ago. This time we were at my house. I had just gotten a new record: "Improvisations," a piano duet with Ran Blake and Jaki Byard. Hayden and I sat on the couch and did what we do: we listened.

Putting Ran Blake, the atonal, nonmelodic, arhythmic, analytic player together with Jaki Byard, the swinging, soulful, hard driving, emotional player is like trying to mix oil and water. This encounter between Third Stream Guru and The Master of Charles Mingus Transmogrified Blues Roots was an instruction in the nature and necessity of voice.

Duke Ellington said, "A man's sound is his total personality."

If the reed instruments are the easiest instruments on which to produce your own personal sound, the piano has got to be the most difficult, yet even on an instrument so unyielding to individual sound as a piano, these two men spoke clearly and distinctly, and separately, as they spoke together out of their vastly different sensibilities and voices. You can't be who you ain't. To quote Thelonious Monk, "How could I be anything other than who I am. A man is a genius just for looking like himself."

One of the ways a musician expresses his or her unique voice is the way in which he or she approaches rhythm. Hayden found somewhere years ago a quote from Max Roach saying, "Every change in the history of jazz has been a rhythmic change." One of the general threads running through all our twenty years of listening together has been our attention to rhythm, cadence, location of the beat, listening for and talking about the rhythmic complexity and subtlety that any African-based music always has. One of the things that creates a distinctive, individual sound, a voice, is how a particular player approaches the beat, and one of the great sources of surprise and delight in all of jazz is listening for that approach, how he or she will attack the beat, lay back from it, get in ahead of it, shy away from it, steer it, be steered by it, overpower it, give in to it.

Third. Five years ago. Hayden was headed east from Syracuse to do a reading at New England College in Henniker, New Hampshire, where our mutual friend Joel Oppenheimer—who is now dead these almost two years, God rest his soul—was teaching. On his way, Hayden stopped by my place and picked me up so that I could travel with him to the reading. It would be nice, we'd have a few days together with not much to do but hang out, visit Joel and the vivacious and beautiful Teresa, and do what we always do when we get together: listen to music.

We got on Interstate 89 in Montpelier and headed for southern New Hampshire, then promptly got off the interstate at the first exit—both of us being well sick of years of high-speed, interstate driving—and slowed the trip down to a leisurely toodle through the valleys and along the rivers that lay between us and our destination. And as we drove in that insular privacy a car in motion affords, we listened to music. I don't know how long it took to make that trip. However long it was, it wasn't long enough.

First that day we listened to Hayden's beloved Sidney Bechet. Hayden had introduced me to Bechet years before. In my early days of listening to Bechet I did not appreciate him. I came to musical consciousness during that time in the mid-1950's when BeBop was in full bloom, and to my BeBop ear Bechet's music sounded too much like the Dixieland I had already learned to hate for its clichéd phrases and pat emotions. On closer examination, however, and in the care of someone with the depth of knowledge and concern Hayden has for music, I had come to see how Bechet and his friends were anything but pat or clichéd. I began to be able to hear the hard-driving passion of Bechet's playing, his relentless emotional intensity.

Then Hayden played an album by Odetta, who I'm sure just about everybody thinks of as a folk singer. On this album, however, Odetta sings the blues. And again here was a musician fairly exploding with emotional intensity and drive. Odetta's verbal and rhythmic articulation is so sharp and cutting it is almost menacing. Her songs are full of the painful openness of the blues:

> Ain't it hard to stumble
> when you got no place to fall.
> I said, ain't it hard to stumble
> when you got no place to fall.
>   Stranger here, stranger everywhere
>   I would go home, but, Honey, I'm a stranger there.

But full also of political content:

> Oh, Mr. Rich Man, Rich Man
> Open up your heart and mind.
> Mr. Rich Man, Rich Man
> Open up your heart and mind.
>   Give the poor man a chance.
>   Help stop these hard hard times.

> While you're livin' in your mansion
> You don't know what hard times mean.
> While you're livin' in your mansion
> You don't know what hard times mean.
>   Poor man's wife is starvin'
>   Your wife a'livin' like a queen.

And we drove on toward Henniker and toward Joel and Teresa, listening and then talking and then listening some more.

Fourth. A couple of months ago. Hayden was in Vermont for a few days and we had only a short afternoon together. Charles Simic had given Hayden a video tape of a Danish program about saxophonist Ben Webster. If there is any one Black musician who has joined Hayden and me together over the years, bridged our sometimes quite different tastes, and stood for our common understanding of the place and meaning of Black American classical music in American life, and the meaning of being an artist in America, it is Ben Webster.

After nearly twenty years of the two of us listening intently to Webster in all his moods and manifestations, it was a delight to sit down and actually watch the man move through the world, and to *see* and not only hear him play his horn. I was struck, for example, with how often he took a breath and therefore how brief his phrases were. This was a surprise to me since his playing is so liquid and seamless. It was also interesting to see this "old" way of breathing now in a time when practically all reed players can circular breathe and therefore can play one, uninterrupted phrase literally for hours. It was exciting to see this great master use his breathing to "break the lines of his poem" so to speak.

There has never been a player in the history of jazz more willing to express direct, intense and unabashed emotion than Ben Webster. He was never stuck in that sophisticated idea that the expression of emotion is—unsophisticated. And there has never been in the history of the tenor saxophone a player more capable of coaxing out of his horn a broader range of sounds, and I am not forgetting the innovations of John Coltrane, Albert Ayler and David Murray to name only three. In short, nobody more than Ben Webster has produced a more human sound, a sound closer to the human voice in all its many moods and timbres.

As Gil Evans put it, "All great music has to have a cry somewhere; all players and all music—they have to have that cry." No one cried more completely or included in his repertoire a greater range of cries—cries of anguish, sadness, silly joy, sexual ecstasy, hatred, sarcasm, rage, grief—than Ben Webster. In the richness and variety of his tone, Webster was able to express, as Ellington said a player must, his total personality and, I would add, the full range of human emotion.

III

What has struck me in writing these memories of listening to music with Hayden is how much talking about the music we listen to is like talking about Hayden's poetry.

First, the kind of lovingly detailed observation of our world and ourselves and the infinite variety of moods and situations we and the world find ourselves in that is so clear in all of Hayden's work comes from an ability to focus upon the object, mood, emotion and give it a kind of Zen-like attention. This ability to *listen* to the world both outside and inside the self and then attempt to articulate what you hear is rife throughout Hayden's work. As Vietnamese Buddhist Thich Nhat Hanh says, "While doing the dishes, one should only be doing the dishes." Hayden has the ability in all his work to do the dishes.

Second, Hayden has great ears. Where else among American poets is there a writer with a better pair? Whether it be the patois of northern Vermont, in one of Hayden's monologue poems, as in this excerpt from "Lady" from *Brothers, I Loved You All,*

>   One time I was spreading
> manure down in the lower pasture, next the spruces.
> I was late, see, past sundown, because I can tell you
> I got to run seventy minutes to the hour to work

this place. And of course that had to be the time
the damn spreader jams, so there's nothing to do
but throw out the stuff by hand. I was just climbing
off of the tractor with the dung fork in one hand
when this old she bear come out of the trees. Popped ... ,

or the character Amos in *The Sleeping Beauty*

Maybe because they're so damn frigging rich,
Or maybe for shoving some farmer off his land
Or the townfolk out of their housen, them which
Has come down hand to hand
For generations. So they get in a twitch
All proud and feisty-like, and it makes them itch
To buy more, and buy and buy and buy
Till they own most everything. That's why
They think they own the people too, and by God
They do, at least a good cross
Section of us. Hell, you stick a big enough wad ... ,

or the banter of people trapped in the strip-developed suburbs surrounding Syracuse,

Let me tell you, Mac, it's sure great
    seeing you again, I
kid you not. Like old times. You're look-
    ing fine. The reason why

I ain't been around is because
    I moved out. After that
by-pass I had down to Upstate
    Medical. Nothing flat

is how long it took me to get
    down the pike from Liver-
pool, soon as they handed me my
    pension. Sure looked like cur- ... ,

wherever Hayden goes he takes his good ears with him. He can play what he hears.

Third, throughout all of Hayden's work lives an existential and life-giving *defiance*, a resistance, that is healing. Surely all of *The Sleeping Beauty* qualifies here as does the book with the telling title,

Contra Mortem, which ends with the lines,

> and thus we are   Thus on the wheel we touch
> each to each a part
> of the great determining reality   How much
> we give to one another   Perhaps our art
> succeeds after all our small song done in the faith
> of lovers who endlessly change heart for heart
> as the gift of being   Come let us sing against death.

And also this from "'Sure,' Said Benny Goodman," from *Tell Me Again How the White Heron Rises and Flies Across the Nacreous River at Twilight Toward the Distant Islands*,

> Do you remember the Incan
> priestling, Xtlgg, who said,
> "O Lord Sun, we are probably not good enough to exalt thee," and
> got himself
> Flung over the wall at Machu Picchu for his candor?
> I honor him for that, but I like him because his statement implies
> That if he had foreseen the outcome he might not have said it.
> But he did say it. *Candor seeks its own unforeseeable occasions.*

Such as, for another example, one afternoon in Belgium in 1957 when Vic Dickenson let loose and also told the truth.

But perhaps the greatest act of defiance is the simple and dogged avowal to keep singing no matter what, which is what Hayden does in "All Things" from *The Oldest Killed Lake in North America*:

> The music of October
> is the wild geese in the night
> that bring me to rediscover
> above the citylight
>
> how all things are a song
> unmeaning but profound
> and fundamental to the tongue
> we speak here on the ground.
>
> St. Harmonie, let me sing
> the music of October
> in my loquacious stammering
> till all hell freezes over.

Fourth, Hayden's voice is as distinctive and individual as any writer alive. Who else ever writes remotely like him? This individuality of tone, whether it be regarding Ben Webster and his saxophone or Hayden Carruth and his poetry, cannot be illustrated or explained. The uniqueness of the tone is the accumulation of an infinite and undecipherable variety of elements; it is a mystery, and the qualities of it can only be pointed to. Yet through it all we know it is there, and just as somebody "with ears" can tell you in the second bar of the tune whether or not the player is Ben Webster, so also we can tell Hayden's tone instantly. The examples from the poetry to be cited here are: the collected work.

Fifth, rhythmically. In a time when too many white poets are still trapped — after all these years when they could have learned something from the Black writers and musicians all around them! — still trapped in their tight-ass, up and down cadences in the world's most boring 4/4, Hayden's work is as complex, various and interesting as the best African American music. The variety and complexity of Hayden's rhythms seem practically infinite:

> Reverting still again to the hatch from a
> safe distance maybe it was like this
> an engine idling with internal fire
> the bones of the mastodon burning in the
> red light of its lost imagined heart
> 			(from "Reverting Still Again,"
> 			*From Snow and Rock, From Chaos*)

> Ruthie? That's you? Well, how's it go-
> 	ing back there, good? Yeah. Look,
> the reason I'm calling, you got
> 	your ma and me all shook
>
> with that last letter, see? I mean
> 	it's great to get a let-
> ter from your only daughter a
> 	couple times a year; set
>
> us up real good, that stuff about ...
> 			(from "Phone," *Asphalt Georgics*)

The moon was like a full cup tonight,
too heavy, and sank in the mist
soon after dark, leaving for light

faint stars and the silver leaves
of milkweed beside the road,
gleaming before my car.
>(from "The Cows at Night,"
>*From Snow and Rock, From Chaos*)

Just when I imagined I had conquered
nostalgia so odious, had conquered Vermont and the half-dozen
    good years there,
here you come singing "A Cottage for Sale," which is a better than
    average song as a matter of fact, though that's
not saying much and it's been lost to my memory for years and
    years,
but you always had good taste, meaning the same as mine.
Oh Maxine, how screwed up everything is.
>(from "Letter to Maxine Sullivan," *Heron*)

The window
          the icicle
                    the gleaming moon
when the lamplight fails.
>(from "North Winter," *For You*)

Knock off that hincty blowing, you Megarians,
I got a new beat, mellow and melic, like
warm, man. I sing of heisty Herm.

'Twas early dawn when somebody smashed the stars
and hardnose Herm was born. He lay there
on his cot a while, then he raised up and said:

"Ma –" that's Maybelline "– Ma, who's my daddy"? ...
>(from "A Little Old Funky Homeric Blues
>for Herm," *If You Call This Cry A Song*)

    Sixth, since the very beginning Hayden, like any good jazz or blues singer, has, bless him, been incapable of separating art and politics. And never is the political removed in his art into a world unto itself where one might get the misimpression that the political can be abstracted out of our common, daily lives; rather the political is always and forever in the context of the personal and the natural. In poems such as "In Russia" from *Dark World*, or "The Spanish Civil War" and "The Birds of Vietnam" from *From Snow and Rock, From Chaos*, we see politics in the context of its wounding of the earth and its creatures. This is "When Howitzers Began" from *Brothers, I Loved You All*.

> When howitzers began
>   the fish darted downward
> to weeds and rocks,
>   dark forms motionless
> in darkness, yet they were
>   stunned again again
> stunned
>   and again and
> again stunned, until their
>   lives loosened, spreading
> a darker darkness
>   over the river.

Always the political act in the context of the world in which it is acted, in the context of our lives. This is the first stanza of "Song: The Famous Vision of America" from *The Oldest Killed Lake in America*.

> A long sweep
> of prairie to the mountains,
>   distance made clear
> in green grasses colored
>   with yellow, with blue,
>   the wide sky over all,
> and at night somewhere out
>   there in the wind
>   moving gently
> the lynched man hanging from his tree.

And in the face of all this engagement and protesting, Hayden maintains his usual refusal to engage in false hope or pie-eyed dreaming. At the end of "On Being Asked to Write a Poem Against the War in Vietnam" and after making a list of all the wars he's protested he says:

> and not one
> breath was restored
> to one.

In a time in which not only do Councils on the Arts and Senators censor artists, but artists shamelessly censor themselves by declaring in one way or another that art and politics don't mix, it is informative and necessary to attend to the political commitment in Hayden's work. And it is important and necessary to remember, or begin to notice, that everywhere else in the world art and politics are inextricably linked. The President of Czechoslovakia is a playwright.

Seventh, in all of Hayden's work there is an unsurpassed and unabashed freedom to be openly and expressively, intensely emotional.

> I am a fool and all
> men are fools. I know it
> and I know I know it.
> What good is it to know?
>
> (from "Loneliness," *If You Call This Cry a Song*)

> O bright, swift, gleaming
> in dusky groves,
> I mourn you.
> O mindless, heartless, I can't
> help it, I have so loved
>   this world.
>
> (from "The Birds of Vietnam," *From Snow and Rock, From Chaos*)

It is very difficult to illustrate this aspect of Hayden's work with a couple of short excerpts. One needs the whole poem, especially the longer ones like "Loneliness" and particularly "Mother" from *Heron* which ends:

> I see you now in your eternal moment that has become mine,
> You twisted, contorted, your agonized bones,
> You whom I recognize forever, you in the double exposure,
> You in the boat of your confinement lying,
> Drifting on the sea as the currents and long winds take you,
> Penitent for the crime committed against you, victim of your
>   own innocence,
> (Existence is the crime against the existing),
> Drifting, drifting in the uncaused universe that has no right
>   to be.

Here is something Mercer Ellington said about his father that I think applies wonderfully well to Hayden's poetry. "Ellington sought a sensuality in the way his music was expressed; there was an *emotion* attached to the sound.... He was always very conscious of the need to make the listener *feel* experiences with sound." In short, as with our friend, Ben Webster, nobody more than Hayden has produced a richer human sound redolent of all its many moods and timbres.

And finally, eighth, it should be clear in Hayden's work that his poems come to him, he hears them and then writes them down, and clear also that what he hears comes into his ear and goes straight to his heart. In other words, he does not make the mistake of using his head so much that his ears fall off. I have to admit that I get a kind of perverse pleasure and feel a bemused charm in being able to say this about the most scholarly, most erudite, most knowledgeable and intellectually rigorous poet alive!

IV

I have deliberately avoided talking about or referring to the legion of poems and prose pieces in Hayden's *opus* that refer directly to or grow specifically out of his experience with jazz and the blues. Those pieces are self-referential and I thought it better to dwell on the musical influences in general and in poems, for the most part, not directly connected to the music.

Finally, in a piece about Hayden's and my years together listening to music and about Hayden's poetry, it seems only meet and right for Hayden to have the last word.

This is from the last of the "Paragraphs": it is February 12th, 1944, New York City, the W.O.R. Recording Studios, a session to record *Bottom Blues* and "five men knowing it well   blacks & jews" swing into the tune. And where is Hayden?

           Ah,
        holy spirit, ninefold
I druther've bin a-settin there, supernumerary
cockroach i' th' corner, a-listenin, a-listenin, , , , , ,
than be the Prazedint ov the Wuurld.

Clearly, somehow, he *was* there.

V

And now, I announce and declare
before the muse and all of youse
that as of this moment
our friend and fellow poet:
  HAYDEN CARRUTH
is to be christened and crowned
from now on and forever
  THE SUPERNUMERARY COCKROACH
and that the duties and obligations
concomitant with and connected to
this office shall be that said poet
  HAYDEN CARRUTH
shall
for all of us and forevermore
go on
a-settin there
a-listenin, a-listenin

and then playin' what he hears!

David Weiss

An Interview with Hayden Carruth

CARRUTH: ... and I went into the Army during World War II and I wrote some poetry while I was there, too. When I got out I had the GI bill, and I went to graduate school at the University of Chicago because I didn't want to go to work, and there suddenly everything opened up, and I began to read Eliot and Pound and Williams and Stevens and people like that whom I never had heard of before. And also writers of that period, writers of my own age. There were a couple or three good bookstores in Chicago at that time and I used to go there and buy little magazines and things like that. And so I began writing seriously. By then I was 25 years old. My first published poem was in 1946, I believe, and I wrote a lot then. I had some poems accepted by *Poetry*, and I was invited downtown to have lunch with the editors, and I became a member of the staff and eventually became editor. So by that time I was stuck.

WEISS: By that time you had a sense of vocation?

CARRUTH: I had a sense of vocation. So I think of my early years when I was living in the country in a little town and not getting a very good education as a preparation. I think the desire to write poetry was there. I was just terribly ignorant at the time. I didn't really know what I was doing.

WEISS: What made your sense of vocation? What did you feel poetry could do that made it worthy of a vocation?

CARRUTH: Well, I think the sense that we all had in the middle part of the century was that the great poets of the modernist period had made changes in our lives and in civilization in general. It wasn't until later that we began to be concerned with what the solution was. In 1935–1950 we felt that—I can remember Alan Tate saying one time that what he and his generation had wanted to do, hoped to do, was to move American education off the dead center it had been on since Cambridge in 1870. And that, in fact, is what they did. The modernist poets entered the curriculum in universities and even in high schools and the terrific emphasis on Longfellow and Whittier and Lowell was abated, settled. And we felt that that was progress, we felt that something had happened, that poetry had made this happen, that people were consequently more aware not only of poetry but of life in general. I don't know that in the long run it made all that much difference, but that's the way we felt then, and I felt as a young poet that that was what I would aspire to do. I would write poems that would be good enough and strong enough to make people move, to change their minds.

WEISS: Do you still feel like a modernist?

CARRUTH: No. I got over the modernists a long time ago. In fact I think I was one of the first who began criticizing the new critics and modernist writers in general back in the 50's, early 60's. There were a lot of things wrong with the modernists and in my prose writing, in my criticism, I was pretty clear about it. In my poetry I wasn't so clear. I really didn't know how to write poetry that wasn't modernist. All of the business I've associated with energy and function and form and so on that I picked up from Pound and Eliot became my working habits, and it's hard to find your way out of that. I'm not sure I ever did, but younger poets have now.

WEISS: You mean you gave up being a modernist in the sense that poetry has no efficacy in the world anymore?

CARRUTH: I was forced to give up that idea. The people who affected me the most when I was in my twenties and early thirties were the mid-century European existentialist writers, and they had this idea of engagement or responsibility that I believed in and still do believe in. One of the things that was wrong with the modernists was that they tried to get away from reality in the period between the two wars. Some of them were explicit about it, like Gottfried Benn in Germany and Wyndham Lewis in England, and others were not explicit but they were doing it anyway. They were trying to create some kind of an imaginative world that would be saner and safer and more bearable than the actual one. Then came the death camps and all the terrorism in the late 30's and 40's. And people like Sartre said you don't create an imaginary world, you write about the real world. That's been the guideline of my work. I have never been a poet for poetry's sake. I never have been able to do that. I was raised in a family where my grandfather and my father were both newspapermen and professional writers, and always they insisted on the social utility of writing. I can remember sitting in my father's office, he was the editor of a daily newspaper, and when I was six or seven or eight years old, watching him at work pounding on his typewriter with three fingers the way he did and wearing a green eyeshade and sleeve guards, smoking a cigar; he was pounding away at the typewriter and he suddenly looked up at me and he said, "Don't ever take any job that isn't a service to the community." I can remember him saying that to me ...

WEISS: Milan Kundera has said that in the West, God gave way to culture, and now culture has given way.

CARRUTH: That's a big, broad statement but I think that it certainly has a lot of truth in it. That's what the modernist movement tried to do: replace conventional faith with the imagination, and culture with works of art. It failed. Now I see a lot of struggling and exploring and experimenting among younger folks, my students, for example, and I don't see anybody that's got a clear vision of the right thing to do, but at least they are trying to find some other way.

WEISS: "North Winter" ends, "Winter is the vacancy that flowers in a glance wakening compassion and mercy and/lovingkindness north is the aurora north is deliverance emancipation .../... north is nothing." All human and moral values seem to derive from this emptiness, this abyss. Has this remained true for you?

CARRUTH: Yes. Very clearly. When I was writing "North Winter"

I was also writing a book about Albert Camus called *After the Stranger* and it was the first winter I spent in the North country, and I went out for a walk each day and by the time I came back I wrote down a little note, and then at the end of the winter I realized that these notes had some coherence so I edited them together and wrote that, the "Afterward," I think it's called; it comes at the end of the book. I was thinking a great deal about freedom and responsibility and the difficulty of the human being who has no faith, no support in a metaphysical sense. Life is absurd, yes. There is nothing, there is no underpinning, there is no over-intelligence: the human being makes his own way by resisting and by denying, by disacquiescence, and sustains himself as a human being with some kind of human dignity in spite of chaos and absurdity. So those are the things I was thinking about when I wrote that poem. And so they got into it. I think I still feel that way, basically. Many of my friends, it seems lately, have become religious people in one sense or another. I've had some discussions with them about it. I just don't see it. I don't like it.

WEISS: You think it has something to do with the exhaustion that comes with the continual work of self-creation?

CARRUTH: I think that has a lot to do with it. Also, the exhaustion of living in the nuclear age. All the terrors that we have all the time. The end of the world is now a real possibility. People have been writing about it since the beginning of time and it has usually been a vision like some kind of a terrific violence, recently atomic, but now it's just what's happening when you look out the window.

WEISS: "The Incorrigible Dirigible," the first poem in *Tell Me Again How the White Heron Rises and Flies Across the Nacreous River at Twilight Toward the Distant Islands,* ends with these lines, "such a magnificent, polychronogeneous idea, flight by craft that is lighter than air!/ I hope it will be revived." Do you think of this as a figure for the poem itself?

CARRUTH: I did at the time that I wrote that poem. Most of my concepts have sprung up spontaneously and in an impromptu way and many of them I throw away. I do believe in that quality of just taking anything, coming out of anywhere, out of any topic or any object and making it float, making it shape itself in such a way that it will go. That is what poets do in our time. That is necessarily a fragmentary process. We don't believe in masterpieces anymore and I don't think we should. We don't believe in the Great American Novel. We used to talk about it all the time when I was young. The Great American Novel is never going to be written or it's going to be a compendium of a hundred novels written by a hundred different people.

WEISS: In this notion we have come a long way from the 40's and its idea of the perfectly made gem.

CARRUTH: Yes, we have. I think we've had to get rid of that idea. That was the modernist hangover from the 19th century, I think. The idea that a poet like Yeats or Eliot could produce a work that would be self-enclosed, autonomous, and famous—kind of a monument—we had to give that up. It just didn't work. In a world of terrorism and war and all the rest of our problems that kind of poem was irrelevant. It's a museum piece and as working poets, as writers, we have to engage ourselves more in the chaotic situation that we live in. A lot of things have happened. One of them is certainly the emphasis that the Theorists with a capital T put on the deconstructability of the text and the inability of the language to represent contemporary reality and so on. Ideas like that are very damaging to the modernists. But we live with them now all the time.

WEISS: "Before a man can create a poem," you once wrote, "he must create a poet." What did you have in mind?

CARRUTH: I don't remember writing that and I don't know really what I had in mind at the time. But, a poet has to be somebody who is sensitive and has some kind of a vision. Even a very amorphous vision. The reason that most of the kids that are coming along now are not poets is because they don't have that. They don't have any sense of goodness. To me, poetry and goodness are almost synonymous. They go together, so in order to be a poet, you have to have a vision at some point. As a product of the 20's and 30's, the depression and all that sort of thing, I have that. I also believe that the real poem, and I've said this many times, the real poem is not what's on the paper, it's what occurs in the poet's mind, in his imagination, before he starts messing around with language.

WEISS: So the creating of the poet is a prior activity?

CARRUTH: Frequently the imaginative process and the writing process go hand in hand and you don't conceive the whole poem until you've written it. But before you sit down to write, you have to have an imaginative field of knowledge and feeling of what you want the poem to be like. Usually you have some sense of timbre or texture, something like that. The relationship between imagination and reality is something that's important.

WEISS: Do poems begin with a hurt?

CARRUTH: I think all poems begin with a concern. They may begin with a hurt. I think the concern is prior. You have to have that. If you are not concerned about something then your poem is going to be empty.

WEISS: You have always been concerned with philosophy. Is that a matter of idea or language? What is the distinction between poetry and philosophy?

CARRUTH: Well, it seems to me that in the most fundamental sense both the poet and the philosopher are aiming at the same thing. The poet works with his imagination, the philosopher works with his reason. That's very arbitrary and the fact of the matter is that poets work with reason and philosophers work with imagination. The extent to which I can write specifically on the topic of philosophy has varied from time to time. When I was writing the *Heron* poems, I was reading Schopenhauer and enjoying it a good deal. What Kant was trying to do when he wrote the *Critique of Pure Reason* was to explain something, explain how we function, who we are, and I think he did it very beautifully. It's out of date now, and no longer are we able to believe that he had his finger on truth with a capital T, no more than anyone else. But I think of it as a poem basically. Something I like to read for the way he orchestrated his ideas. In that sense philosophy has been very important to me.

WEISS: You say the following thing, and I wonder if it's similar to what you think is common to the philosopher and the poet. "The poet's task is to fashion a new image of man in his own time."

CARRUTH: Well, that was an idea that was common among the modernist poets and new critics. That certainly is part of what the poet does—give back an image to the reader to enable him to see himself in his own contemporary predicament, and that's part of what the philosopher does too.

WEISS: Does *Asphalt Georgics* provide such an image, satirically?

CARRUTH: Yes. I don't think of it as being satire very much.

WEISS: You think it's a kind of verisimilitude?

CARRUTH: I think it is, and I hope the poems in that book have a kind of sympathy. There's a certain sense in which I am making fun of the people in *Asphalt Georgics*, but I hope that the reader gets the idea, the feeling, that I'm making fun of myself just as much, that we're all in the same boat. Speech patterns have always interested me a lot. While I was writing those poems I intentionally carried a notebook around which I don't normally do. I copied down things that I overheard in diners and restaurants and bars and places like that and then I'd go home and work them into a poem. I wrote most of those poems fairly easily and I enjoyed writing them. From the very beginning I always liked to write against a relatively difficult, technical program of some kind. I invented those poems when I lived in Liverpool, N.Y., near Syracuse, in 1981 or 1982, because I felt I was in such a changed environment from anything I had lived in before, and I thought my poetry ought to change too. I had written syllabic poems before but never of this kind, and I sat down one day soon after I got there with a tablet of paper and I began writing down numbers and things like that and I came up with a simple, little syllabic stanza with perfect rhymes, and they seem to have evolved out of each other; one poem suggested the next one and then I exhausted it. That's what has happened to me many times in my life. I got tired of writing the syllabic lines. The sonnets (*Sonnets*, The Press of Appletree Alley, 1989) were written in a period of about a year and a few months and I wrote five or six a day sometimes; other times I went a couple of weeks without writing any. I came to the point where I didn't want to write any more sonnets. So I stopped. The long-lined poems in the *Heron* book were also written in a period of about a year and a half and I got tired of writing those also.

WEISS: How different are your "paragraphs" from the sonnets? When you started writing sonnets why didn't they turn into fifteen liners? Is it purely the rightness of the arbitrary? Or is it a matter of structure?

CARRUTH: I think it's a question of my relationship to the tradition. When I wrote the sonnets I wanted to write a sonnet sequence based on sex and romance in the great Renaissance tradition. The fifteen liner, what I call a paragraph, is my own. I invented it and used it a number of different times. I used it for *The Sleeping Beauty* because I thought of it as my poem, my personal form. I suppose the reader doesn't notice much difference between the paragraph and the sonnet, one extra line and a slightly different rhyme scheme, but I do think that there's a difference. When I first invented the paragraph, I was influenced by a sonnet of Paul Goodman that I published in *Poetry* magazine when I was an editor in which he displaced the final couplet and put it in the middle after the octet and followed by a quatrain, and I liked that. I thought it changed the sonnet, gave it a kind of a pivot in the middle. So when I invented the paragraph I put a rhymed couplet in the middle, a tetrameter couplet, and in a way the whole history of what I did with the paragraph was to get around that terrible barrier, that terrible problem I'd given myself, because having a rhymed couplet in the middle tends to break up the poem terribly and I had to find ways to flow through that.

WEISS: And you felt the necessity of retaining that difficulty?

CARRUTH: I'm stubborn as hell. I did it from the beginning.

WEISS: "Tradition is not convention. Tradition is always unexpected/ like the taste of the pomegranate, so sweet," you wrote in "My Father's Face."

CARRUTH: Well, I think that's true. I think that the tradition is alive and it is always surprising. When you run into it, it does have the quality of novelty. That seems to be paradoxical in a way because it is attached to things in the past. But as a person who is very interested in jazz music, I have always been fascinated by the problem of how you can tell that a record made in 1950 by a group of good musicians has the spontaneity and originality that a record made in 1960 by other musicians who are influenced by the first ones and who are imitating them, doesn't have. I have no solution to that problem. I don't know how to explain it, but I know; I can tell when the musicians on a record are doing something new and original and fresh and spontaneous and when they're not. Even though the imitation ten years later may be very, very good, it doesn't have the same quality. And that's the tradition, the tradition does that. I teach prosody to a certain extent. All kinds of prosody, not just conventional English prosody, but other kinds, too. It seems to me that the most important function of prosody, of meter, measure of any kind, is not to establish a rhythm for the sake of the rhythm itself, but to let the reader or the hearer anticipate what's coming, the next beat. And that kind of propulsiveness, that's the tradition. Meter serves the same function in a poem that tradition serves in literature in general. It is what allows us to see what's coming next, anticipate the next phrase, the next phase, the next evolution. I think that's a fair analogy.

WEISS: Would you use measure and meter interchangeably? It seems measure is something more—many of the lines in your poems which are not strictly syllabic, strictly accentual, or strictly iambic, have measure. The sense of measure doesn't seem to have to do exactly with that.

CARRUTH: Well, I use the term in different ways, at different times, and that's part of the inconsistency. Fundamentally, though, I agree with you. My sense of measure is much bigger and it doesn't even apply to poetry to a certain extent. You know in Langue D'oc, the language of the south of France, *mesura* is the word for wisdom. Aristotle said the same thing: wisdom consists of a just perception of measure. But when I'm teaching prosody I use the term to indicate the meter, the beat, or the actual rhythm in that particular line.

WEISS: In one poem, Paul Goodman writes, "Through the brilliant curtain of July,/I spy the way whereon we deviate,/but do not err." Something about both deviating but not erring has to do with the large capacity within an ideal like measure.

CARRUTH: Deviation is what we invent. The way we get to where we go is the invention. And it needs limits. It needs the tradition. It needs something. Jazz musicians have discovered that you can improvise in infinitely extraordinary ways, but almost always it works best if it's based on a simple meter and a simple figure. A simple melodic structure. Musicians who have tried to improvise in what they call complete freedom without anything in their minds to control the way the improvisation goes have not been so successful. And I think it's the same in poetry. I have to have limits at any rate when I write, and that's one of the reasons why I sometimes write in syllabics. You can't hear syllabics in English. It's simply a compositional aid for me and I like that sense of working against a frame or a scaffold or whatever you want to call it. I think probably in most of the long-lined poems in *Heron* there is a certain consistency from line to line. Not a fixed number of beats by any means, but they are not extremely different. I'm not the kind of poet who writes long-lined poems with very short lines stuck in there. The rhythm in those poems is controlled by syntax, by the flow of ideas, by the mood I'm interested in. In very much of my poetry I am conscious of pace, the speeding up or slowing down, keeping the beat but at the same time creating a tension against the beat through fast and slow passages. I think that's at work in the long-lined poems just as it is in all of the others.

WEISS: I think particularly for the long-lined poems the word *pace* is good because one feels a kind of gait that remains steady no matter the terrain you're passing over.

CARRUTH: I think that's true. As a person who has been a musician and very interested in music, I think for me, personally, the beat is the beat and as Count Basie said, "No cheating." Four to the measure and no cheating. Well, I feel that way. Obviously the analogy of poetry to music is a little dangerous, but for me the beat is the beat and I stick to it. If I create a long line that's got 9 or 11 beats in it, that's what determines the line breaks. The pacing of the line is determined by vowel sounds to a certain extent, by the difficulty or ease of the consonants, and especially by the placement of unaccented syllables. How many you have together in one place, how few you have and things like that. At Syracuse University, to the extent that I teach anything, I try to teach the—I don't like to use the word tradition and I don't like to use the word convention—I like to teach the young people something about what I call the company, the assembly of great artists: great poets, artists and philosophers. Take Alexander Pope, for instance, a very important poet. When I was learning, when I was a kitten, I studied his versification, I tried to imitate it, but more than that I found him a person whom I admired tremendously and I still do. Here is a man who, before the Romantics ever came along, helped invent the first poetic persona in a way that had never been done before as far as I know. Here was a man whose life was absolutely miserable and crippled, no sex, nothing. So whatever life he had, had to be in his poetry. Between his early poems and his late poems he turned himself into a presence, a real presence in the poems. And that presence is as important to me, was as important to me as a young writer, as the actual poems themselves. The quality of his imagination flows out from the poems like an aura, and the energy, the love – these poems are written in love. Most people don't realize that and I think that is very important. Young poets can attach themselves to a dead poet in that way. I don't know how many of them do it, but it is possible.

WEISS: What you describe sounds like a relationship of apprenticeship.

CARRUTH: Very much. I remember when I first came to Syracuse and first went to work as a teacher, I had a conversation, as everybody has to, with the Dean. The Dean was a chemist and he said to me, "Well, what do you think about teaching?" And I said that I feel the way to teach would be to have the teacher or maybe two teachers or three teachers and a few students living together and running a farm. It would be similar to the apprentice/master relationship that existed in the studios of painters during the Renaissance, for instance. I got a surprising response from him. He said, "That's true. It's the same way with chemistry. The most learning takes place in the laboratory, not in the classroom, where the teacher and his assistants are equally engaged in a project of some kind. There is basically an apprentice/master relationship between them and it is informal. That's the way chemists learn the most." I thought that he was perceptive and I still think that. There's no way that anybody has figured out how to do this within the structure of the academy. But I try to push my workshops in that direction, if possible.

WEISS: How did you turn out to be such an inveterate neologizer? Whether it's prefixes or suffixes or a word like *bestowal* from the Brahms cigar poem or *furiosity* or *vanishment* or *verbigeration*. They all feel inspired, outlandish and, most of all, wonderfully appropriate at that instant.

CARRUTH: Well, the only thing I can say about that is that they come spontaneously and I think when I do that there's a little crisis. If you're a jazz musician and you are improvising, you're blowing along on your horn and you come to a point where something is just too difficult, you don't know what to do, so you just blow as hard as you can and make a sharp noise. Hope that it works.

WEISS: Well, that's a good explanation for it. It mostly does work. I think of it as a kind of witching stick; it's something that just shoots down to some improbable configuration of syllables.

CARRUTH: I think that poets of my age, basically, and older poets too of the twentieth century here in America, have been lucky because the condition of the American language in the twentieth century has been similar to the condition of the English language during the Elizabethan Period and the Tudor Period. It's expanded. Neologisms are a part of the popular imagination. There's a lot of wonderful slang that's been invented during our time, which is necessary. It sticks; it fills a need. There weren't any words there to do it before. Technology and so on obviously was also pumping vocabulary into the language all the time, so that we have an inventive attitude toward language and I love that. I love to be on the street and listen to kids talking, especially if they're kids who are black or Puerto Rican, any group that has a subdialect that has at least a potentiality of replacing standard English. I've always felt that some of the best writing, a lot of the best writing, comes from the fringe. It doesn't come from Oxford or Cambridge, it doesn't come from Harvard. It comes from Ireland, it comes from Nigeria, it comes from the south in the United States, it comes from the edges where people feel a lack of language. The language is not rich enough for them and their conditions are changing so they've got to have new words and then give new meanings to old words, all kinds of things like that.

WEISS: A lot of your neologisms have a wonderfully archaic feel. I don't know if archaic is the right word, but they feel etymologically rich.

CARRUTH: I think I have always been interested in old language as long as it's lively and has something going there. I love to read seventeenth century prose. I don't read very many sermons and I don't read political tracts, but there are a few books, prose books, from that period that I think are just wonderful. Things like Aubrey's *Brief Lives* and *Pepys's Diaries* and Bradford's *History of the Plymouth Plantation*. Those writers make up grammar, they make up syntax, and they make up their vocabulary as they go along.

WEISS: Robert Pinsky has written in his recent book *Poetry and the World:* "To imagine an American life, American poetry characteristically—maybe inevitably—begins by imagining, implicitly or explicitly, its own unrealized place in that life."

CARRUTH: I think that's an acute formulation of a problem that we all deal with all the time. I just finished writing a review for a magazine. One of those big quarterly round-up things, and most of the poets, all of the poets in the review except one, are living American poets. The other is Yannis Ritsos. A number of things stuck with me as I was reading that distinguish Ritsos from the American poets. One of the things, strangely, is that Ritsos is not influenced by Catullus as everybody else in Europe and America is. I don't think I would have noticed that if I hadn't also been reviewing a new translation of Catullus at the same time. More important, Ritsos so obviously lives in and has lived all of his life in a social, political, and cultural environment that was active and in which he participated as an active agent, and it gets into his poems, even poems that don't have anything to do with politics. Every poem of his has a kind of, what I call, applicability that our poems don't have in this country. In our country we don't have that. Not just poets, but most Americans live in a kind of political torpor. We feel helpless. The kind of changes we know ought to be made are not being made. In our poetry we tend to turn away. We all work in the knowledge that we're not producing any effect on our civilization. The politicians and the powerful people in our country conduct their operations and their lives without any reference to art at all. In other places, that's not true.

WEISS: At the close of "Paragraphs" you say you'd rather be a "supernumerary/cockroach i'th'corner .../than be the Prazedint ov the Wuurld." What would you do if you were "Prazedint ov the Wuurld?"

CARRUTH: Well, I would put things right. God knows how. I think people of good will and intelligence all over the world know what's wrong, know that the evils in the world are basically derived from greed and the desire for power. That kind of thing can be legislated against. That's what I would do if I were a politician. I would legislate against the greed. Legislate against people living off of other people. There's nothing new about that. Aristotle said the same thing. Certainly not on the scale of the world or even of the nation, but communal enterprises at one time or another throughout history have worked. Most people of intelligence and good will have been interested in it. Basically that was what Ezra Pound was interested in. He was interested in a banking system which didn't have any usury. And he wrote about the historical examples of that happening. There weren't very many of them and he got to be cranky and kind of crazy. We have here in Oneida a pretty good example of a nineteenth-century utopian community, the Oneida Community. Organized first, I think, after the Civil War, they believed in communal living to a very large extent, even to the extent of communal marriages. Consequently they raised a lot of people's eyebrows. But they succeeded, for a long time anyway, and they succeeded financially too because they founded the Oneida Community Silverware Company, which is still profitable. Things like that are hopeful.

WEISS: After legislating against power and greed, would you then outlaw legislation itself?

CARRUTH: Well, I would. But I'm what you used to call a philosophical anarchist. I don't have any illusions that real anarchism is going to work on a large scale. I do believe, however, that freedom is the basic goal, and in political activity you try to move in that direction. I know that in my life, a sense of sympathy for suffering people began very, very early and where it came from I'm not certain. It may mean that I had been injured myself in my childhood. I can remember, though, when my family got the first radio that we had, which was perhaps 1927 or '28, being in tears because of things I heard on the radio that other people didn't pay much attention to. I remember especially a terrible, terrible program called "Major Bowe's Amateur Hour." It was during some international fair in New York back around 1930. This was an ordinary amateur program where people came on and did their turn and if they weren't good enough the Major would bang a bell and interrupt them and chase them off. So they had an African guy from the fair who came and who couldn't speak any English and didn't know anything about American culture; I doubt if he even knew exactly where he was, but he was a fine drummer, a wonderful percussionist on the African instruments, and he began to play. He was doing what he did and the major laughed and the audience laughed and the major banged on the bell and this poor African guy got dragged off the stage, and I wept for hours after that. I just could not believe that anybody could be that cruel, that barbarous. That was in me. I don't know where it came from, it was in me. It's always been.

WEISS: I think of that section in *The Sleeping Beauty*, the 53rd, in which you're thinking about the Cuban revolution in relation to the poet Ernesto Cardenal, "who loves [the] revolution, the equalities,/the courage, the beautiful new nation." But then you say, "Cardenal *saw* the camps, saw the oppression,/Cardenal saw the State ... ." You then call yourself, "still a boy-anarchist," and add, "They say: choose./But Spirit he cannot, he can't. Then what shall he/Do?/Nothing./He'll be. And he'll sing the blues." That's an awful yet necessary position to have to be in. In this poem, you are unable to affirm this change because of the suffering it has caused.

CARRUTH: Yes. That's true. I have always thought of myself as radical and a person who wants radical change. I still do, but the idea of suffering that has to go with it is more powerful in me than the desire to see that change, I guess, especially since so often the change is not a change but simply more of the same. But it is a tough question, and when I say that there is nothing to do but sing the blues I'm saying, in effect, that the existential situation of the individual in the 20th century is such that probably the only real outlet is in making something. It doesn't have to be a poem, it doesn't have to be music, but it has to be something imagined, something created.

WEISS: It was Camus who said that either you can be on the side of those who make history or on the side of those who are subjected to history, and a writer must be on the side of those who are subjected to the forces of history.

CARRUTH: In that sector, in the sector of political thought and feeling, he was more important in my life than anybody else—although I had read a lot of radical literature when I was young, including a lot of anarchist literature. What I say in the poem is true. I did become an anarchist to the extent that one can become anything at the age of fifteen, when I read an account of the meeting of the International, the First International in Brussels, I think, in 1870 or so, when Marx and Bakunin split over the question of the dictatorship of the proletariat and the takeover of the state.

I still believe that. Basically I've gone through Lord knows how many changes and shifts in attitude and judgment since then, but basically I still think that the ideal is freedom, that both the community and the individual should be moving toward freedom even though they never can reach it.

WEISS: There's a passage at the end of *Sitting In* which in its visionary hope reminds me of Whitman. It's not a "Prazedint's" hope; clearly it's a poet's:

> I don't know what a poet's dreams are worth – maybe not much. But I dream continually of a great session where race, or more properly speaking, ethnicity, has no significance at all, where "culture" is irrelevant, where every performer and listener participates freely and equally in the bodily and spiritually wrenching, exhilarating, purging experience of jazz-in-itself.

CARRUTH: Well, this is a prose statement that is very parallel to a section in *The Sleeping Beauty*. I don't think I have been influenced by Whitman much. But yes, I do think art in general has that capacity if it is recognized in its greatness. It's the source of freedom. There is no freedom as such in the real world, in existence. One has to transcend existence to find freedom, and one does that through the imagination, or at least it can be done through the imagination. The individual becomes existentially free when he is using his imagination in some kind of transcendent moment. In the real world you are determined, you can't avoid it. You are determined biologically, you're determined historically, socially, politically, and economically, and every other way. When you are living within your imagination and your imagination is active, all of these determinants fall away and you become existentially free, and at the same time you come into some kind of sympathetic understanding with other imaginations which are also existentially free. How this happens exactly is something that is mysterious to me, but it does happen. That kind of freedom and that kind of imaginative activity is to me the richness that we are capable of as human beings and very, very important to me. I've written about it a lot, but this section from the *Sleeping Beauty* expresses it, I think, in one sense, the same as the end of *Sitting In* does:

> In the mind's house of heaven, the great night never
> Ends.
>   All the brothers are there: Berrigan, Bechet,
> Russell, Hawkins, Dickenson, Hodges,
> And Mary Lou and Lady Day,
> And so many others.
>   And oh they play, they
>   jam forever,
> Shades of strange souls nevertheless caught together
> In eternity and the blues.
>   No need
> To cut anyone any more, no fatigue
> From the straights out front or the repetitive changes,
> But only expressiveness,   warmth,
> Each invention a purity, new without strangeness
> In that session.
>   Always they strained on earth
> For this thing, skin and soul to merge, to disappear
> In howling sound.
>   God, but it would be worth
> Dying, if it could be done,
>   to be there with them and to hear,   *to hear.*

NOTES ON CONTRIBUTORS

Wendell Berry's most recent books include *The Hidden Wound, The Remembering, Home Economics,* and *What People Are For,* all from North Point Press.

Philip Booth's new collection of poems, *Selves,* has just appeared from Viking.

David Budbill's play *Judevine* was put on by A.C.T. in San Francisco this past winter. *Why I Came to Judevine* (White Pine) is his most recent collection.

W.S. Di Piero's new collection, *The Dog Star,* will be out this year.

Geoffrey Gardner has recently edited the selected poems of Paul Goodman for Black Sparrow.

Sam Hamill's most recent books are *Basho's Ghost,* essays on Japanese poetics, and *A Dragon in the Clouds,* poems and translations in the Zen tradition, both from Broken Moon Press. *A Poet's Work: The Other Side of Poetry,* literary essays, will appear this year.

Geof Hewitt lives in Calais, Vermont, and works in the State Capitol for the Vermont Department of Education. Ithaca House has just published his second book of poems, *Just Worlds.*

Carolyn Kizer's most recent collection is *The Nearness of You* which appeared in 1986 from Copper Canyon.

Maxine Kumin's most recent collection of poems, *Nurture,* was published by Penguin in 1989.

Stephen Kuusisto is just completing his first collection of poems, a number of which have appeared in *Antioch Review* and *Quarry West,* among others.

William Matthews's most recent collection of poems, *Blues If You Want,* came out from Houghton Mifflin last year.

David Rivard's book, *Torque*, won the Agnes Lynch Starrett Prize from University of Pittsburgh Press in 1988; he teaches at Tufts.

Anthony Robbins is a poet. He lives in Duluth, Minnesota.

David Weiss's first collection of poems is *The Fourth Part of the World* from Ohio State.

SENECA REVIEW

Deborah Tall, Editor
Hobart & William Smith Colleges
Geneva, New York 14456

Available Back Issues
$3.50 each

Vol. XIII, No. 2. Feature: Poems and an interview with English poet Andrew Harvey. Poems by Heather McHugh, David St. John, Stephen Dunn, Ann Lauterbach, Hilda Morley, and others. Essays by Dave Smith and Jonathan Holden.

Vol. XIV, No. 1. Translations of Rilke, Akhmatova, and from classical and contemporary Arabic poetry. Poems by Rosanna Warren, Carol Frost, Jane Kenyon, Eric Pankey, Walter McDonald, Luis Omar Salinas, Geraldine C. Little, and others.

Vol. XIV, No. 2. Feature: Poems and an interview with Stephen Dunn. Poems by Christopher Buckley, Linda Gregerson, Laurie Sheck, Debra Nystrom, Michael J. Rosen, and others. Essays on Ellen Bryant Voigt and Charles Wright.

Vol. XV, No. 1. Arrowsmith translations of Montale. Levitin translations from the Portuguese. Poems by Charles Simic, Stephen Dobyns, Peter Sacks, Maura Stanton, Myra Sklarew, Gary Soto, Elizabeth Spires, Susan Stewart, Jordan Smith, Albert Goldbarth, Judith Kitchen, and others.

Vol. XV, No. 2. Guest-edited by Stephen Dobyns. Poems and an interview with Thomas Lux. Poems by Ellen Bryant Voigt, C.K. Williams, Ray Carver, Bill Knott, Steve Orlen, Mary Karr, and others.

Vol. XVI, No. 1. Special International Issue. Poems from the Catalan lands, the Middle East, and Asia. Irish poet Eavan Boland.

Vol. XVI, No. 2. Feature: Poems and an interview with David St. John. Merwin translations of Roberto Juarroz. Poems by Seamus Heaney, Rita Dove, Jared Carter, Susan Stewart, William Heyen, Patricia Goedicke, David Wojahn, and others.

Vol. XVII, No. 1. Poems by Gregory Orr, Mekeel McBride, Donald Finkel, Cleopatra Mathis, T. Alan Broughton, and others. Eight Upstate New York Writers. Translations from South America. Mary Karr on "Missing Larkin."

Vol. XVIII, No. 1. Poems by Robert Pack, Carl Dennis, Molly Peacock, James Reiss, Maurya Simon, Barbara Goldberg, and others. An essay by Stephen Kuusisto on Japanese poet Nanao Sakaki.

Vol. XVIII, No. 2. Poems by Cornelius Eady, Robert Farnsworth, Brooks Haxton, Richard Frost, C.S. Giscombe, and others. Translations from the Bengali and Japanese.

Vol. XIX, No. 1. Poems by Hayden Carruth, William Matthews, Patricia Goedicke, T. Alan Broughton, Sharon Bryan, and others. Translations of Yannis Ritsos, Raúl Barrientos, and Galician-Portuguese Troubadour Poetry.

Vol. XIX, No. 2. Feature: Contemporary Polish Poetry—an interview with Stanislaw Baranczak and a selection of poems translated by him and Clare Cavanagh. Poems by Denise Levertov, Cornelius Eady, Vern Rutsala, Diane Glancy, Gerald Early, Carol Frost, and others. Translations of Jules Supervielle, Max Jacob, Angel Gonzalez, and Mihai Eminescu by Geoffrey Gardner, Rosanna Warren, Steven Ford Brown, Pedro Gutirrez Revuelta, and W.D. Snodgrass.

Enter my subscription for _____ year(s). (Rates: $8/year; $15/2 years. *Seneca Review* is published twice yearly, spring and fall.)

Send the following back issues for $3.50 each: _____

(40% discount to bookstores.)

Make check payable to *Seneca Review,* and mail orders to Deborah Tall, Editor, *Seneca Review,* Hobart & William Smith Colleges, Geneva, NY 14456.

Name_____

Address _____